TWICE
UPON A TIME

TWICE UPON A TIME

by
Paul Keens-Douglas

POETRY & SHORT STORIES

Cover design: **Marlon Nicolls/Ken De Peana (Markens)**
Illustrations: **Dunstan E. Williams. (DEW)**

Published by:
Keensdee Production Ltd.
21 OLD PADDOCK ROAD, BLUE RANGE,
DIEGO MARTIN, TRINIDAD, W.I.
1-(809) 632-1647

Other works by Paul Keens-Douglas can be found in his publications: **When Moon Shine, Tim Tim, Tell Me Again, Is Town Say So, Lal Shop,** and on L/P Albums **Tim Tim, Savannah Ghost, One To One, Fedon's Flute, Is Town Say So, Fete Match, Bobots, More Of Me,** and **Carnival Is Marse** . . . All are available from the publishers.

Copyright ⓒ 1989 by
Paul Keens- Douglas

Printed in Trinidad by The College Press

ISBN 976−8069−05−8

A WOMAN

Figures tumble through life's mystery
Flashes of light at dusk . . . the past
That speeds across my staring eyes,
Seeing a force that enfolds all,
Gentle but strong, the loving wrap of care
Entwined with folds of understanding,
A woman whose very life bore me
Uncomprehending, as a bottle on the waves.
I not looking back, eager to be gone
Beyond the known, to live my life my own
Yet with ear bent ever back for fear
I lose the force which gave me speed,
I caring, but not showing, taking for granted
The things, the units of my life.
And suddenly, softly I turn to look
Back down the winding road of me,
And I can see far, far away at the end
Where my footsteps begin, a glow,
A woman whose hands stretch outwards
Still holding me from falling into darkness
With pillars of love borne on silent prayer.
My mother stands a lonely bridge
That spans the gap, my life to death
And she awaits me at both ends
With understanding . . . .

When Moon Shine 1975

DEDICATION

Boy, yu mean to say, you dont know
yu mother die last night?
Oh . . ah sorry . . ah thought yu knew!
Dats how I know dat Mommy dead,
Ah phonecall, break of day,
An' I, tinkin' was de usual,
Answer de usual way.
Wha' ah could say, but tank yu,
Ah go' call home right away.
An' so ah did, quite calmly,
An' shock dem wit' me voice,
'cause when it come to spreadin' news,
Niggergram is de natural choice.
She had jus' gone to bed, gone to sleep,
An' continue on she way,
No farewell, no goodbye,
No we'll meet again some day.
Jus', "Don't wake me in de mornin', Temps!",
Meanin', "When yu miss me ah gone!"
An' so said, so done,
Is we to ketch an' mourn.
But not to worry, not to fret,
De lady had she way,
Dats de way she wanted it,
As she used to tell us every day.
"Son", she say, "You may come one day,
An' yu ole Mom may not be here,
So gimme what yu givin' now,
Ah cant spend it over dey!"
An' so ah give she wha' ah had for she,
An' she give me she gentle smile,
Ah blessin', when ah tink 'bout it,
Dat made everyting wort' de while.
An' so ah went to funeral,
We bury she in style,
But to me she still 'upstairs'
An' will be 'down in a little while!'

Contents

CELEBRATING US

Paul Keens-Douglas celebrates our rich cultural amalgam and Caribbean landscapes like nobody else does. With a bubbling well of humour and humanity and heart, he reaches into the innermost crevices of ourselves and our cultures and produces a unique, necessary, sensitive and endearing happy-making and deep thoughtfulness that bring us back to joy, feeling, to the real sweetness of our societies, to the serious history of our legacies, to people real people and to loving our own. In the midst of the terrors and dreadness of our bloody pasts and presents, economic dependencies, struggles, Keens-Dee reminds us of the real warmth, depth and sugar-appleness of our complex little communities, of our lovely darknite peoples and our fun-filled nation languages capable of all emotions. He celebrates us. And we laugh at it all from our very toes.

Particularly in Trinidad vernacular, shaped and carven by his own special Grenada/Caribbean/Diaspora sensitivities, he records for today and tomorrow the interstices of our lives; the tiniest, human, real, people-pulsing, hilarious, sad, tender, mauvais langue, picong, tolerances, pain and plenty of our lives. Everybody has loved a rambunctious "Tanti Merle", brought up a wind-dreaming Vibert or lived through one, knows a "Slim", forever "steupsing", no teeth and all, and worshipped at the magic of the steelband music of a "Sugar George" . . . .

Despite the failures of our politicians and politicking, the exploitations and rip-offs by others and ourselves, the back-bends of poverty, the "break-words" and bitterness of underdevelopment , all of which he includes with deft and sometimes light touch, Paul Keens-Douglas makes us laugh, makes us remember, makes us recognise and claim the matrix of our subterranean strengths which make us able to go on.

He creates a new era in the oral tradition and more praise-songs should be sung of him. For laughter is the gift of the gods and goddesses we must never lose. He reminds us that "Laughter like ah wish — ah wish for understanding" and that "each story have two ending" — "odder people view and our view". "An ' every seat had two people .. one inside de other. An ' one was laughin ', de other crying' " . . . . The Yin and the Yang of us. And of our societies. Too often in the utter hilarity of his work, many forget to see the quiet philosophical side of this poet expressing in his own gentle way, the deepest feelings, committments, anguish, insights, perceptions. He feels "we cant make before we time" . . . "we're growing." And our societies are growing, despite the doom and gloom which is often very real. As we live in the peripheries, in the dread pressures of centre imperialisms, he makes us remember the unique and beautiful, enduring qualities of our basically, relatively gentle, makoshash, oblique, clever, scrunting, insular, tender, deceitful, wonder-ful, prejudiced, kaiso, busing, worldly and street-wise, kiff kiff peoples and our amazing surviving islands; that in Trinidad produce a Carnival, the miraculous steel-bands and spin-offs of such creativity, it is unbelievable with all its strangulations and a friendly, welcoming Tobago-ness that the world is forgetting.

From outside eyes, the Caribbean is a dream space, a mecca, a spiritually unique, sociological "baedeker", a vital, musical and magnetic center, a riviera, a paradise; a cross-roads of world cultures, a fantastic polyglot, with all its problems, its eviscerations, a harmony of hope, a new world, a new age black diaspora amalgam of immense possibilities, potentials, creators, rhythmic powers, in a magical setting of sun and sea we forget to remember to see. Paul Keens-Douglas 'wide-ranging' work reminds us. Celebrates us. Makes us remember. When the thousands throng his performances, we celebrate ourselves. We see ourselves in close-up and know it is true.

Essentially a Caribbean synthesized voice, he reminds us as we laugh, of the Caribbean Dream and reality. Stressing the positives instead of only the dark histories. As oblique in his criticisms as we ourselves in our boundary-maintenance societies, his rapier wit makes us guffaw at our weaknesses and our strengths, our histories and our own human foolishness, gossip-ridden lives and potential for gleeful, malicious little savageries. We can listen to him for hours, marvelling at his memory, his control, his apparently effortless professionalism, the simple connection of a man with his audiences he holds contentedly and skillfully in his long expressive tapering hands. For he is always showing us ourselves, **exactly** as we really are, our foibles and our deep and abiding capabilities for compassion, irony and for loving. When he says "I Love You Island", he is voicing what we forget to remember, to say . . . .

So I think of Paul Keens-Douglas' work as a celebration. A celebration of our cultures, of ourselves. At once he is a museum himself and is creating museums of our pasts and presents and our futures. He captures us for our memories. To hear the school-children gleefully rendering and learning his work, alive, themselves and cavorting with joy, is to witness and understand the shaping of time. He tells the world and history that our underdeveloped societies didn't only suffer. His people are our people, household names. He is the wide tapestry of us darknite folks ever growing at the edges. To really understand the full significance of his prolific work and what it means in the literary tradition growing out of the West Indies, is to know that at the start of this very century, work like his, totally indigenous (like Miss Lou, and Mikey and Dobru and Kamau and Marley, Rapso, Malik, Binta, Sistren and many others now) would have been totally impossible. He is part of the Black Diaspora voices exploding. He would, like the others, be unheard of. And unsung. Cecil Herbert, one of Trinidad's earliest and finest poets, recorded bitterly in his time of the twenties and thirties, "Whoever heard of a 'nigger' poet?"

In the welter of colonialisms for those who managed to get to school at all, Chaucer and Shakespeare, Keats and Shelley were the only way to go. It was Sparrow's, "Dan is the

Man in the Van" time. Rhyme and the iambic pentameter ruled the poetic roosts. To be educated was to be British, French, Spanish, Dutch, elite . . . . with the languages of the colonisers as first and ruling tongues. The Voice of the Folk of the People was not recorded. Nor respected neither. But it told tales and sang, stories and song from dark-night to dawn, day-clean, in every crevice of our tiny, black, ridden socieites. Then largely hoed the canes and cocoa in silence. Work-songs were allowed. Sometimes. And so the oral tradition grew. But not to repeat the vital points, many of which I support, already made in the other several prefaces to Paul Keens-Douglas' other five books, I want to move and to record here the importance of his work and art as part of the growing, creole, indigenisme edge of our oral traditions and to place it squarely in the context of NATION LANGUAGE, the Voice of the Folk of the Caribbean.

Edward Kamau Brathwaite, our Path-Finder and Houngan of History and Assortor Drum in W.I. Literature Professor of Cultural History at the University of the West Indies, in his HISTORY OF THE VOICE (1984) says:

"It is NATION LANGUAGE in the Caribbean that, in fact, largely ignores the pentameter. Nation Language is the language which is influenced very strongly by the African model, the African aspect of our New World/Caribbean heritage. English it may be in terms of some of its lexical features. But in its contours its rhythms and timbre, its sound explosions, it is not English, even though the words, as you hear them, might be English to a greater or lesser degree . . . . . .

. . . . it is an English which is not the standard, imported educated English, but that of the submerged, surrealist experience and sensibility, which has always been there and which is now increasingly coming to the surface and influencing the perception of contemporary Caribbean people. It is what I call, as I say NATION LANGUAGE. I use the term in contrast to **dialect**. The word "dialect" has been bandied about for a long time and it carries very perjorative overtones. Dialect is **thought of** as "bad English". Dialect is "inferior English". Dialect is the language used when you want to make fun of some-one. Caricature speaks in dialect. Dialect has had a long history coming from the plantation where people's dignity is distorted through their language and the descriptions which the dialect gave to them. Nation Language on the other hand is the **submerged** area of that dialect which is more closely allied to the African aspect of experience in the Caribbean. It may be in English; but often it is in an English which is like a howl, or a shout or a machine-gun or the wind or a wave. It is also like the blues. And sometimes it is English and African at the same . . . ."

He notes further

"In the Caribbean our novelists have always been conscious of these native resources, but the critics have, as is kinda often the case, lagged far behind. Indeed until 1970, there was a **positive intellectual almost social, hostility to the concept of "dialect" as language**. But there were some significant studies in linguistics . . . ."

What was called "dialect" has become freed today, freed of the perjoratives as people claim themselves and their languages as their own vehicles of themselves. **There is a new naming,** a statement of **nommo** as the imprisoned free themselves of history's sneers. In the absence of the above nomenclature, NATION LANGUAGE, we now make ourselves, Paul Keens-Douglas has been called a "dialect" poet. He also, like Louise Bennet and Mikey Smith and many others across the Caribbean and Black ‚Diaspora in a variety of forms, has removed the term "dialect" from the colonisers down-grading connotations and the neo-colonisers (read also as W.I. snobbish, semi-educated, sometimes academic, elites) smirks and smears. It is why Paul's work is so widely appreciated and loved across the Caribbean, his shows always over-flowing and packed with joyful audiences, his popularity growing in more and more areas of the diaspora, in the USA and U.K. and in student performances and studies and academic theses on far-flung campuses.

It has been no easier for the snobs and some academics to accept his work in parts of the West Indies than for them to accept the kaiso and reggeh also as art forms, as poetry. That also took its time. But today Trinidad's best-known calypsonian the Mighty Sparrow is now "Dr Sparrow" after a UWI award of an honorary doctorate for his inimitable (if often smutty, woman-denigrating and colonially apolitical) genius. We ourselves can do the laughing (and crying) at ourselves without the denigrations or distortions when handled with honed sensibilities. And recognitions come; Paul Keens-Douglas was invited as Special Guest Artiste of the 40th Anniversary Celebrations in 1989 of the University of the West Indies held at the Mona campus, Jamaica where art is reverred and national contributions understood.

In Paul Keens-Douglas we have an internationally-acclaimed Caribbean artist with a trained sociological observer eye and ear and a warm heart which loves his islands shamelessly and out loud and often; full of joy and caring, mischief, irreverence, whimsy, honesty, working within his own integrities and distilling and developing from a base right here in the Caribbean and the dialect/nation language as art form; recording the ever-changing W.I. lifestyles in a very particular type of engaging and entertaining form of story-telling. He shows, with his business-like, organised approach to his art, that artists can survive on their own ground and do not have as in the past to become permanent exiles. While a lot of his work is done abroad like many artistes still, he is part of the growing artist population rooted at home and letting down the bucket right here at the navel-string. It comes from being about your own business in your own tongue and fighting to do in on home ground. His professional and careful management of his business in every respect demonstrates to other artistes that it can be done. His early detractors, the inevitable "tearer-downers" of our societies, fall silent as book after book (now six), recordings (now nine) after performance, TV programmes and Caribbean-wide radio programmes and invitations to appear attest to the growing quality, depth and appreciation of his work. In his recent 1989 Trinidad performance at THE LITTLE CARIB with Geraldine Connor LRSM, musician par excellence as his guest artiste this time, he moved his work even closer to the Caribbean's musicality of tongues which is its base. In closing duet they interwove folk-song and haunting cadance into story. And one remembered the lilting beauty of the semi-sung FEDON'S FLUTE . . . . . .

This Trinidadian-born, Grenadian bred poet-singer, story-talking in Caribbean feels

"To be what one is
Fulfills the essence of existence" . . . . (WHEN MOON SHINE 1975).

Every artist has his/her own views of the world and they make him/her unique. One has but to keep polishing the spirit and the craft. Whatever structures and forms he chooses to express his sensitivities to his culture are intrinsic to who he is. It is the multifarious, creative forms we produce in the W.I. that make it so rich and fecund. It is not enough to fall into the latest popular modes, be it revolutionary or rapso, valid as they both are. Each artist, inside the hounfort of his/her culture and selfhoods finds true voice and crystallizes and develops the craft to express it. It is the road to authenticity and new creative, innovative developments. Paul Keens-Douglas is himself. He never pretends to be any other person. And it is one of his strengths. Any uneveness is part of his human growing, learning, erring, moving on. Being himself, he is not the overt revolutionary voice but the glancing, humourous, pointed exposure of the details that breed revolutions and celebrate a culture to be preserved and loved, against all odds. Too often as we shake with laughter or gleefully smile we forget to look at the serious areas and contribution of his work.

And there are many. As they say, his unforgettable work is "too numerous to mention". Pieces like "Sugar George",

"Savannah Ghost", "Fedon's Flute", "Sugar-Apple People", "WukHand", to name a few are still to be given the proper analysis and attention they so richly deserve. Indeed it is part of the problem facing not only Paul's work, but that of many other "new wave" writers and artistes. Where to find the critics with the essential insights, experience, grounding and tools to examine the new work being produced now out of our polyglot black cultures. The hope is that as the years unfold and the new writers and artistes come into their own, so too will a new breed of critic emerge, capable of understanding, appreciating and doing justice to the new horizons blossoming and exploding on our landscapes of Caribbean literature and art.

In the meantime the work goes on, and in Paul's case, before the sternest critics of them all, his public. And the fact that they have supported him and continue to do so, is the greatest tribute that can ever be paid to his work. And now comes TWICE UPON A TIME. And since you now have it in your hands, I will leave it to you to enjoy the endearing and enduring talents and sparkling wit of Paul Keens-Douglas. It's another Celebration.

marina ama omowale maxwell
Writer/Lecturer/TV Producer & Director
Commissioner (Caribbean) of the Schomburg Center (N.Y.) for the Preservation of Black Culture.

THIS AN' DAT

Ah once met ah English poet,
Ah West Indian . . yu understan ',
One ah dose who always claimin;
How, "We take over de Motherlan' ".
We was both waitin' on taxi,
An ' dis man nearly get me mad,
Because jus ' so he start discussin ',
Culture in Trinidad.
Well, I tell him ah was ah poet,
An ' how ah does use de vernacular,
Well you would ah swear dat I cuss dis man
Or insult he granmudder.
Dat man start talkin' language,
Like he wukkin' BBC,
Or he head de English Department
At we University.

If yu hear him.

This dialect you fellows talk about,
It really has to go,
You're all just Neo-colonials,
An embarassment to us who know.
Such a limited language,
If language is the word,
It seems more like garbled English,
The worst I have ever heard.
English is now our language,
It's no longer the Englishman's,
Like cricket, we now control it,
Do try to understand.
Why should one preserve this dialect,
So frivolous, it's just a fad,
Always changing, no vocab,
It's simply speaking 'bad'.
It isn't even standardised,

It goes each and every way,
Some call it 'native language'.
The 'vernacular' others say.
What use is speaking dialect
When you have to go abroad?
Or speak at some great conference?
They won't make out a word.
You chaps mislead the people,
By holding up on high,
A base part of our culture,
That should be quietly left to die.
Think of names like Milton,
Prospero or Caliban,
Think of William Shakespeare,
That's the heights of language man.
But what's this 'dis', and 'dat', and 'dem'
Unless it's just for style,
And if it's just for impact,
It's hardly worth the while.
Take myself for instance,
I've got my PhD,
I can tell the world 'bout English,
At University.
I've got Roget's Thesaurus,
I've got my "Book Of Quotes",
You will never hear me use such words,
As 'wassy, 'scrunt', or 'jorts'.

Same time he flag ah taxi,
Like is dat he born to do,
'English' was more 'Trini'
Dan de likes of me or you.
An' as we start to drive away,
Like sardine in ah pan,
At home wit' de same dialect
Dat he cant understan'.
Laughing' wit' passengers,
Asking' for kaiso,

20

Dey offer him ah 'Doubles',
De man beggin' for more.
An' as ah watch dat goin' on
Ah tink of wha' he say,
An' others jus' like him
Ah meet from day to day.
Dey run so far from dialect,
Yet dey always comin' back,
Like dey always have de feelin',
Dat dey mus' defend de fact.
Dem who crossin' river
An' cussin' river-stone,
Does end up cryin' water,
An' end up all alone.
For when you run from dialect,
Is you runnin' from you,
So de answer is de 'maxim',
To thine own self be true.
So I dont worry take dem on,
I jus' waitin' to see,
When dey find out who dey are
Or who dey want to be.
For dialect dont bother dem,
Is dem dat bother it,
Because dialect, it livin' 'home',
Is dem dat have to fit.

AH DONT WANT TO KNOW

Dont tell me 'bout your problem,
Yu see me? Ah dont want to know.
Don't tell me 'bout de children,
'cause ah go' tell yu ah told yu so.

Dont tell me how yu feelin' sick
But yu 'fraid de hospital,
Jus' fly up to Miami,
Ah dont want to know at all.

An ' so what if de bank eh give yu ah loan?
Or dey take back de motocar?
Nothin ' eh wrong wit ' catchin ' de bus,
An ' foot could still take yu quite far.

Don't tell me 'bout de system,
UWI or CXC,
Dey say is de experts dat runnin ' dat,
So don't come complainin ' to me.

Don't even mention de radio
Or dat ting dey callin ' TV,
Jus ' go an ' call up de Sponsor
Or de Advertising Agency.

So yu gettin ' worried 'bout culture?
Well let me tell yu flat,
De whole place turnin' Yankee
Is really as simple as dat.

An ' so what if dey say pan in danger?
Yu ever see panman at show?
Or Calypsonian for dat matter,
Look, yu see me? Ah don't want to know.

So current gone up sky high,
An ' TELCO jus ' raise up yu bill,
Yu see me? Ah dont want to know 'bout it,
Yu go ' talk, but yu payin ' it still.

Don't even mention de hole in de road,
An ' how it mash up yu motocar,
Jus ' drive round it, forget 'bout it,
Or check out de Minister.

Ah don't want to hear 'bout no vagrants
Or mad people walkin ' round town,
Dey have ah ting call ' Police,
Dat suppose to be takin ' dem down.

People like you don't riot,
Folks like you don't cuss,
Allyu so too decent,
To really kick up ah fuss.

Yu don't support nothin ',
Unless is you dat feelin ' de pain
Now yu have ah problem,
Yu want to confuse my brain?

De Media don't support yu?
De Radio don't play yu song?
De Government ignore yu?
Yu now find someting wrong.

Yu tink is now dat goin ' on?
Man, welcome to de show.
Don't tell me 'bout your problem,
Yu see me? Ah don't want to know

TARA

And so she came
All dressed in blue
Tara Marie that's who!
It's a boy, it's a boy, it's a baby boy
Just like we always knew.
But surprise, surprise, the boy's a girl,
Change the blue to pink,
Call the shop, rewrite the card,
We dont know what to think
We were sure it was a baby boy,
All our dreams were blue,
We even picked a special name
Stewart Anthony Paul — that's who.
But somehow Tara did her thing
And now she's here to stay,

And Stewart will have to wait awhile,
And come another day.
And she took her own sweet time,
Like the woman she's going to be,
As if to give us warning,
I am going to be just me!
As if to say forget that boy
Girls too can bring you joy,
Just wait and see, you'll hear 'bout me
TARA PAULA MARIE!

LIMING

When people talk about the 'sweet sound' of Trinidad & Tobago, the first thing that springs to mind is 'pan' and 'calypso'. That's understandable, seeing as to how Trinidad & Tobago is internationally famous as the birthplace of the Steelband and the home of the wittiest of all songs, the calypso.

But from the moment you set foot in this marvelously mixed-up land called Trinidad & Tobago, and you meet your first Trinidadian or Tobagonian, then you begin to hear that other 'sound' of Trinidad & Tobago, the sound of the people. That in itself is an experience. Because apart from the natural music and rhythm engrained in the intonations of the Trinidadian accent, the native language, the vernacular, the creole, or as some prefer to say 'the Trinidadian use of English', is an adventure all by itself.

In Trinidad & Tobago we have a way of saying things all our own. We have words that have become social events, a way of life. Words that change meaning depending on when they are said, how they are said, where they are said, who is saying them, what tone of voice he uses when he says them, and how he puts his face when he is saying them.

One such word which has become a national way of life is the word 'lime'. When a Trinidadian or a Tobagonian tells you, "Let's go for a lime!", he is not by any stretch of the imagination inviting you to go pick that particularly sour citrus fruit which makes such delicious drinks as Lime Squash, or Rum Punch. What he is talking about, is going somewhere to do nothing or something in particular. He is inviting you to go "Liming".

Liming is the Trinidad & Tobago art of 'hanging out'. But it is more than just 'hanging out'. It is a social event that has different connotations depending on time and space, and different levels of participation. You can go and 'lime' by a friend, in which case you dont dress up too much, as you have no intentions of going further. When you see the girls with curlers in their hair and short-short shorts, and the men with short-pants, hard-calves, and slippers, that's a 'casual lime.'

Now if you are going to 'lime ah fete' or 'party', you dress properly, just in case you get a chance to 'storm' or go in free. Or you might decide to pay and go in, if you find things look on the bright side fete-wise. On the other hand, out of the blues, someone may ring you up and say, "Boy is wha ' you doin ' home all by yuself? Leh we go an ' buss ah lime!" Dressing can be confusing here. because you know that you are going somewhere, but you wont know where till you get there. The best thing to do is put on hard shoes, and walk with a change of clothing. To 'buss ah lime' is the favourite expression of the uninvited and unknown guests.

Then you may be invited to a 'small lime' with just a few people socialising, or ah 'big lime' with plenty action. Then the 'big lime' or 'small lime' may turn into a 'sweet lime' or a 'sour lime', depending on how well things are going. Don't be surprised if your friend turns to you and says, "Leh we split dis scene man, dis lime don't have no juice!" A no-juice lime is definitely a non-event.

Then from a social point of view, you have to be a 'part of de lime' to get invited. Not only that, but everybody has their favourite 'liming hat', 'liming dress', 'liming pants', and 'liming partner, not to mention favourite 'liming spot'.

Now the 'liming spot' is very important, be it a certain street corner, bridge, lamp-post, rum shop, bar, or restaurant. Because depending on where your 'liming spot' is, you may be called a 'social limer' or a – 'roots'. As a matter of fact, some people are better known in terms of their 'liming spots' than their homes. You may occasionally hear someone say something like this, "If allyu lookin ' for George, jus ' go down Frederick Street any Friday 'round four-thirty. Allyu bound to find him. He always by Queen Street corner. If he not dey check by Lal Shop. Dat man dont miss ah 'Friday lime' at all!"

And having said all that about 'liming', ah invitin ' all ah allyu to come to Trinidad & Tobago an ' buss ah lime wit we. De lime sweet too bad, which mean it sweet too good!"

THE EIGHTH DAY

(Narrative depicting the birth of the islands of Grenada, Carriacou and Petit Martinique as performed at Expo '86, Vancouver, Canada.)

Intro: Stage in darkness. Spotlight comes on and focuses on lone dancer, motionless, with national flag in her hands. She does solo dance with flag. Slides of Grenada are flashed on screen in background. Her dance introduces the other dancers who join her on stage and they complete the opening number. At end of number lights fade on dancers and spotlight focuses on storyteller. He comes to edge of stage and addresses the audience.

"Tim Tim . . . . Papa welcome. And how are you my children? I am going to tell you a story, a wonderful story, about a beautiful island, about three beautiful islands in the Caribbean Sea. Oh, they have plenty beautiful islands in the Caribbean Sea, but these three, these three are different, these three are special, especially the one they call Grenada. (Theme Music Grenada in/slides flash briefly)

And why is Grenada so special? Well, that is what this story is all about. Now it's just a story, you hear? So don't go saying how I telling lies. I just telling you what other people tell me. But I don't think big people go ' lie just so, so it must be true. Any way, the way I hear the thing, is like

26

this. (Theme music. Dancers in stylised movement mime the making of the World.)

Once long ago, the whole world was a big, empty space. Then the great Papa God decide to make the Earth and everything on it. It take Him seven long days to do it, so you know was no easy job. He make the sun and the moon and the stars. He make the land, the fruit and the trees. He make the rivers, the seas, and the lakes. He make the animals, the fishes, all the living things. He make all that, and it take Him seven days. Yes, everything on this Earth the great Papa God make in seven days, and on the seventh day he rested. (Dancers freeze. Lights fade)

And this is where our story really and truly begin. It begin with a question. What did Papa God do on the eighth day? Don't worry, if you dont know I will tell you. After all, I am the storyteller, and I know my story. So relax. This is what I hear happen.

On the morning of the eighth day, Papa God get up from His rest and He look around at the wonderful world that He had make, and you know how Papa God eye big already, one look and He see everything. Papa God watch the World for a minute, then suddenly He glance down, and He see that He was sitting down on the top of a big, tall, mountain, on a little, tiny island.

Papa God smile, because you could imagine how Papa God look cock-up on top a mountain, looking like a Piparette bird? That is the same mountain they call Grand Etang today, but I eh reach that part yet, so hold on. Yes man, Papa God smile when He see where He was. And when Papa God smile, was like the whole island begin to smile, and the climate start to come like it was a reflection of Papa God smile. And from that time on to this day, every day is like a tropic day on that tiny island, and every dawn is like the smile of Papa God. (Theme)

Then Papa God reach out He hands miles across the Earth, and He scoop up some of the whitest, finest, purest sands that He had make. And He hold it high, high, admiring it beauty. And as Papa God watch it, He let that golden sand trickle down between He fingers. (Lights on dancers who do flowing motion of sand falling)

And as that sand fall, it twirl and swirl across the tiny island, settling slowly like bands of gold, forming some of the most beautiful beaches in Papa God's entire Universe. In all, the little island was blessed with, they say, 365 splendeferous beaches. One for every day of the year. But the one that everybody does always talk about, is the one they does call Grand Anse. But that is another part of the story. (Slides of beaches etc. .)

Then Papa God stretch forth He left hand, and even as the golden sands trickle through the fingers of He right hand, He dig He left hand deep down into the richest soils of He creation, and He hold it close to look at it. And as He look, He hold it so close, that He breathe on it. And as He breathe on it, it become fertile and full of life. And Papa God laugh, and toss it to the winds, and the winds grab it, and spread it like a blanket in the air, and it fall like fine rain upon the little island, covering it with soil that was rich with the breath of God, soil on which all kinds of fruits and crops could grow. (Slides of Agriculture or dancers miming)

Crops like Bananas, Cocoa, Sugar Cane. Delicious Mangoes, Sapodillas, Guavas, Paupaus. Stately Coconuts. Magnificent Mahogany, Cedar, Pine. Trees and fruits and crops of all kinds began to spring from this God-blessed earth, this God-kissed soil. Especially the ones they call the Nutmeg, and the Spices. That's how come you always hear people talking 'bout the Isle of Spice. But that's another story.

Yes, as I was saying, after Papa God pick up that rich soil and scatter it so generously over the little island, He notice that He hand still had some soil on them. So He decide to wash He hands, yes, the great Papa God decide to wash He hands. And He reach over into the middle of the Earth, and He scoop up a handfull of the purest, clearest, bluest, whitest, cleanest water, and Papa God do so. He wring He hands together. And as He do that, the water run down He arms, and He face, slip through He fingers, and scatter in thousands of drops through the tropical air. (Slides of rivers etc.)

28

And as the drops fall on the island, they form beautiful lakes, and rivers, and pools, and streams, and gullys, and waterfalls. You ever hear 'bout Anandale Falls? And the seas become bluer and clearer, and all kinds of fish and seawater creatures begin to swim 'bout and jump up in the water, the God-blessed water.

Then Papa God look down and around at the little island that had catch so much of He creativity and He blessing, and He smile, and He say, "Little island, us I have rest on you, so too will Man one day find you a restful place, a place of peace and quiet, even in the darkest times. For I is you, and you is Me, and in Me you will always find peace!"

And with one leap Papa God rise straight up in the heavens, in a blaze of light, like a shooting star. But as Papa God leap up from He seat on the top of that mountain, He leap was so great, that two piece of mountain break off, and shoot up into the sky, and fall in the sea, forming two more little islands, even smaller than the one that Papa God had been sitting down on. No need for me to tell you the name of those islands, or the one that Papa God had been sitting down on. Man call them Grenada, Carriacou, and Petit Martinique . . (Music . .dancers portray diff. races)

And as the years pass, man discover the richness of these little islands. Their pleasant climate, bountiful sea, fertile soil and teeming forests. The peaceful Arawaks was the first to come. Then the Caribs, a proud race of warrior Indians. Then the French. Then the English. And they fight each other for the islands. And was endless war and plenty people dead. Till in the end is the English who win. Then, braps! They bring in slavery. They go quite in Africa and bring thousand of Africans to work de land. And more people dead. Because dem African didnt take it easy, was rebellion down de line. Yes, Grenada had plenty rebellion. You ever hear 'bout Jules Fedon and the Fedon rebellion? But that is another story.

Anyway, one day 22nd May, 1838, they abolish slavery forever. But the memory of this history remain in the culture of the people. That's why you could still find them practicing the Shango Religion of Africa and dancing the Bellair and Pique which they get from the French. (Drums start).

But it is in Carriacou that the memory remain the strongest, for it is in Carriacou you find the 'Big Drum'. Unlike some Caribbean Islands, the Carriacou people still maintain their tribal ancestry intact, and many families know from which African tribe they descend. And on festive days when they celebrate big occasions like boat-launching, or giving thanks for good harvests, they dance the Big Drum or Nation Dance. And each family dances only to the beat and the step of its particular tribe, be it Ibo, Moko, Congo, Temne, Mandinka, Chamba, or Kromanti. (Dancers do Big Drum)

You see what I mean when I tell you that Grenada Carriacou and Petit Martinique culture full of history? But that is not all. Is what I doing now? Telling a story, not so? Well you see this thing they call storytelling, is something all Grenadians like, as a matter of fact, all West Indians. In Grenada you find two kinds of stories, the Nanci Stories and the Tim Tim stories. The Nanci stories come from Africa, and in them you find the African Folk-figure of Ananci the Trickster Spider. Ananci always trying to trick people by using their weaknesses, and plenty times he does trick himself through his own weakness.

All the other stories they call them Tim Tim stories, and that come from the French influence, the patois. Because as I tell you before, Grenada used to be French, that's why they have names like Gouyave, Sauteurs, Piedmontemps and Point Saline, and they used to speak plenty Patois once, and they used to begin their storytelling by saying "Tim Tim!" and the crowd would say, "Bois seche!" Like saying 'once upon a time', but not quite. Let me show you what I mean. (Does a Nanci Story. At end of story he exits and dancers do final number based on Anancy. At end they exit. Spotlight picks up storyteller)

Well all stories must come to an end sometime, but how you like that story 'bout Grenada, Carriacou and Petit Martinique? Not bad, eh? But if you dont believe that the great Papa God make those three islands on the eighth day as I tell you, well that's your business. But if you want you can come to Grenada and see for yourself. You will see that that story must be true. Because no where on Papa God Earth, you will find three islands with that special something, that you will find when you come to Grenada, Carriacou and Petit Martinique."

(Music comes up. Dancers come on take bow. Lone dancer with flag enters last. Circles stage. Leads cast off.)

BOTTLE BUSINESS

One night in Chaguanas
Walkin' down de street,
De sound of Tassa in me head
De rhythm in me feet.
When, braps! Ah Indian man,
Like he catch ah sudden light,
Decide to open business,
Dat had me in ah fright.
De man like he get ah message
He should enter into Glass,
An' start exportin' right away,
Jus' as I about to pass.
Now if was glass he makin',
Ah really wouldn't mind,
Because dis country need investment,
Of each an' every kind.
But he main ting was breakin',
Wit' distribution far an' wide,
An' like somebody order bottle,
He had 'bout ten case by he side.
An' when he start to send dem out,
Try an' understan',
Dat man eh wait for boat or plane,
He deliver all by hand.
You ever hear ah bottle fly?
Especially in de dark?
Well dat night ah hear ten thousan',

31

An' dat eh no skylark.
Dat man export some bottle,
You had to be dey to see,
Was like he workin' on commission,
Or he gettin' royalty.
Was bottle lef', an' bottle right,
Bottle high an' low,
Was bottle on people rooftop,
Bottle by dey door.
All dis time I take aside
An' make detour to pass,
Because me eh order bottle,
An' me eh order glass.
Nex' ting bottle comin' back,
Was Import Export now.
Half of dose dat he send out,
Start comin' back any-how.
Some come back whole,
Some come back break,
Some come back like ah joke,
Because he been sendin' empty Coke,
An' he get back some Old Oak.
Ah see some Vat go flyin' by,
Like business turn Ole Marse,
But under all de ole talk,
Not one FULL bottle pass.
Dis time if you see de road,
Like dey pave de place wit' glass,
People walkin' in de drain,
Was de only place to pass.
An' dem piece ah bottle shinin'
Like diamonds in de light,
An' Taxi have to tip-toe,
If dey wanted fares dat night.
Nex' ting ah see de business man
Headin' out ah town,
Somebody send Receiver
To shut he business down.

An' de Receiver bring he lawyer
To show-off in de place,
A brand new, shiny cutlass,
Dat could argue any case.
An' dat is when I decide
To avoid legality,
Because nex' ting dey callin' me
To tell dem what I see.
An' so ah make me detour,
An' ah find ah way to pass,
But I'll never forget Chaguanas,
An' dat man who export glass!

DE DAY ANANCY BEAT PAN

"We gonna tell a story
A story 'bout Anancy
Anancy the Spiderman.
That little tricky spider
Who cross the sea from Africa
And will always try to trick you if he can.

Chorus

Anancy, Anancy,
Anancy, Anancy,
Anancy the Spiderman
Anancy, Anancy,
Anancy, Anancy,
That tricky little Spiderman.

Anancy likes to make you do
The things you really shouldn't do
And he knows just how to
Make you do them too.
He's got himself a trickster's bag
With quite a trick or two,
Anancy's always trying something new.

Chorus

So when you see Anancy
Be sure you listen carefully
To all the things he's going to say to you.
And if you know it's wrong to do
Then do what's right and do what's true,
Just look him in the eye and tell him . . shoooo!

Chorus

DE DAY ANANCY BEAT PAN

Once upon a time, before my time, before your time, before anybody time, all de panmen in Trinidad & Tobago decide to have a contest to see who could beat de bes' pan in de whole worl'. An' as allyu know, Trinidad & Tobago is de home ah de steelband. Yes, man, dat's de place where de steelband was born. But dat's another story.

Anyway, everybody was excited, because de First Prize was ten thousan' dollars an' ah free trip to Egypt to see de Pyramids. Why Egypt? Ah dont know an' dont bother to ask me, ah only tellin' yu de story as ah know it.

So Pan Trinbago, de big steelband organisation in Trinidad & Tobago, make ah grand announcement on de TV. If yu hear dem, "Be it known to all the people of Trinidad & Tobago, that a big Steelband Competition will be held on the first of October, to see who could beat the best Tenor Pan in the whole wide, world. The First Prize will be ten thousand dollars and a free trip to Egypt to see the Pyramids." Now ah Tenor Pan is one ah de lead instruments in ah Steelband. Is ah small pan wit' plenty notes, an' does usually carry de melody, an' yu have to be real good to play it.

Now Anancy, de Spiderman, who come from Africa to de Caribbean wit' de slaves, an' who could do all kind ah tings like change he shape, an' talk in different voices, an' who does always be tryin' to trick people, was sittin' on he roof watchin' de neighbour TV through ah open window. Now remember ah tell allyu dat Anancy was ah trickster. Well, he was also very cheap. Anancy didnt want to spend too much money on electricity, so he used to put off his TV, an' climb up on his roof, an' watch de neighbour TV through de window.

As a matter ah fact, Anancy even used to invite he friends over to watch TV through de neighbour window. He used to tell dem how he have a Drive-In TV, fully airconditioned, an' when dey arrive he used to charge dem five dollars, an' was roof time. Anyway, from de time Anancy hear dat de First Prize was ten thousan' dollars, he say to heself, "I in dat!", an' is enter he want to enter de people competition.

De only trouble was dat Anancy didn't own ah Tenor Pan. So he decide dat de best ting to do was to buy one. But remember, Anancy dont like to spen' money, he cheap. So he decide to ring up all de big bands an' ask how much for ah Tenor Pan. He ring up Despers, he ring up All Stars, he ring up Invaders, he ring up Phase Two Pan Groove. He even get in touch wit' ah band call' Guava Stick Satans who have dey panyard way up on top El Tucuche, the highest mountain in Trinidad. As a matter of fact, is only Anancy who know how to get in touch with de Guava Stick Satans, because dem fellas dont come down town at all, at all. Dem is de last of de 'Badjohn' steelbandmen, an' dey say dey eh have no time wit' no 'Sponsor Band', dey playin' for deyself.

Dem Guava Stick boys real harden yu know, dey does tune pan wit' dey bare hand, ah mean dey hand real hard. Dey does cuff pan into shape. Dey dont use fire, an' hammer, an' tuner, an' dem kind ah ting. Is one set ah cuff in dem pan tail, an' is to hear dem pan soun' sweet. Well, boy, when all dem people tell Anancy how much ah Tenor Pan costin', Anancy say, "Nah, I not spendin' my good money on no pan. I go' get one for free."

Well it so happen dat ah lady name' Miss Cartar had jus' get ah new dustbin from de Solid Waste people, dem people who does collect de garbage an' keep de place sanitary. De dustbin mark "Litter Me." Well Miss Carter decide that she go' do she bit to keep de city clean, an' she start puttin' all kind ah garbage in she new dustbin.

From quite where he was sittin' on top ah coconut tree teafin' coconut, Anancy spot Miss Cartar puttin' out she garbage. Anancy take one look at de new dustbin, an' he say to heself an' de coconuts on de tree, "Dere is my Tenor Pan!" An' as soon as Miss Cartar turn she back an' gone inside, is because Anancy run down de tree, throw all Miss Cartar garbage on de groun', an' take off wit' de lady brand new dustbin.

37

Miss Cartar in de mean time comin' back wit' ah nex' set ah garbage, throw it where she thought de dustbin was; an yu know is because she throw de garbage on de groun'. Ah 'police' happen to be passin', see dat, charge Miss Cartar wit' litterin'. Well is now confusion start, because Miss Cartar now want to know wha' happen to she dustbin, an' was endless bacchanal.

In de mean time Anancy runnin' down de road wit' Miss Cartar dustbin on he head, an' laughin' like he jus' win de National Lottery. He jump two fence an' ah culvert, an' cut across ah pasture. Den he stop to rest under ah Mango tree. An' who yu tink spot him? Brer Monkey. Brer Monkey was on top de Mango tree bitin' mango to see if dey ripe, when he see Anancy wit' de dustbin on he head. Well you know how Brer Monkey farse, an' like to mind people business. He forget de mango for ah minute an' shout out, "But ae, ae Anancy, is what yu have dey? Dat's not Miss Cartar dustbin?"

Anancy almost drop de dustbin when he hear Brer Monkey voice, but he recover quick, an' he answer back as bright as ever, "Miss Cartar dustbin? Yu mad or wha'? Dis is ah brand new steel drum I jus' buy from de oil company. Is ah Barbecue Pit I goin' to make. Is ah surprise for me wife birthday, so dont tell anybody. You is one Monkey mus' get invite to de surprise Barbecue Party. Soon as tings fix up, ah go' send an' tell yu."

Well is nothin' Brer Monkey like more dan to hear dat he gettin' invite to party. So he promise Anancy not to say nothin', an' he gone back to bitin' de people mango on de tree. In de meantime Anancy pick up de dustbin, put it on he head, an' head for a quiet place in de forest where he figure nobody could see him, or nobody could recognise Miss Cartar dustbin.

At last Anancy come to ah big Banyan tree, an' he put down de dustbin, an' sit down to tink about how he go make he Tenor Pan. He had de steel drum which was only recently Miss Cartar dustbin, but he didnt have no tools to cut it to make de Tenor Pan. Because to make de Tenor Pan, he had to cut away de bottom of de drum about six inches from de top, an' tune up de top. But to do dat he needed certain tools. So he sit down dey rackin' he brains to figure out how to get de pan cut.

Suddenly Anancy hear somebody whistling comin' through de forest. Who yu tink it was? Brer Mongoose! An' what yu tink Brer Mongoose had in he hand? A brand new hammer an' chisel. Well from de time Anancy spot de hammer an' chisel, he get a bright idea. So he shout out, "But ae, ae Brer Mongoose, is where yu goin' wit' dat rusty ole chisel?

Well yu know Brer Mongoose have ah bad temper. He get vex immediately an' tell Anancy, "Brer Anancy, yu better ketch yu fallin' self. Dis is ah brand new chisel, made in de greatest part of Great Britain. So hush yu mout', an' mind yu business!" Anancy hit back wit', "Greatest part of Great Britain? Boy yu dont know Britain on de decline? Ah bet yu chisel cant even make ah dent in dis ole, rotten, dustbin!"

Well is now self Brer Mongoose get vex, he shout out, "Oh yeah? bring yu dustbin here let me mash it up for you." An' Brer Mongoose take up he hammer an' chisel, an' wit' all de strength of he vexation, start to rain blows on Anancy drum. Bam! Bam! Bam! An' everytime he hit it he bawlin', "Take dat! an' dat! an' dat!"

An' dat is exactly what Anancy wanted him to do. Because every time Brer Mongoose hit de drum Anancy turn it. Mongoose hit it, he turn it. Mongoose hit it, he turn it, Mongoose hit it, he turn it, an' before you could say "Tim Tim," Brer Mongoose cut off de whole top of de steel drum. An' dat is exactly what Anancy wanted.

When Brer Mongoose see de top of de drum fly off, he hold he belly an' he start to laugh. If yu hear him, "Anancy, boy, is like yu go need ah new dust bin. Ha, ha. It serve yu right. Yu should ah never laugh at me new chisel. Ah tell yu dis chisel make in de greatest part of Great Britain. Ha, ha. But dont take it too hard. De best ting to do is to throw yu dustbin in ah dustbin," an' is down de road he gone, laughing at Anancy.

All dis time Anancy fakin' an' playin' how he vex, but from de time Brer Mongoose get out ah sight, he pick up de top of de drum, an' start to dance an' sing at de top of he voice, "Mongoose tink he hold me, but he dont know is I hold he!" Yu have to get up early, to put one on Anancy." After a while he queit down an' begin to tink of what he goin' to do nex'. He suddenly realise dat although de pan cut, it still have to tune. An' it not easy to tune ah Tenor Pan, yu have to get ah expert, an' expert does charge money. An', of course, Anancy dont want to spend no money.

Now de only place he know where he could get ah pan tune in ah hurry, is way up on El Tucuche by de Guava Stick Satans. Dem is de fellas who does tune pan wit' dey bare hand. . But yu have to be real brave to go up by dem witout ah invitation. Anancy decide to take ah chance, because he had to get de pan tune right away.

So he take de pan top, throw way de bottom part, an' head up El Tucuche. When he reach up dey he enter de Guava Stick Satans Panyard. He was frighten, but he only studyin' 'bout gettin' de pan tune. When he see de set ah tough Bad-johns in de yard, he feel like turnin' back. But it was too late. Dey spot him. An' everybody surround him. De leader óf de Guava Stick Satans was ah fella about eight foot tall, an' weighin' 'bout three hundred pounds. An' he was de smallest.

He pick up Anancy by he collar, an' he growl, "Wha' yu want up here!?" Anancy brains start to work overtime, if yu hear him, "Ah come up here for allyu to tune ah pan for me. Ah hear allyu is de best pan tuners in de whole of Trinidad & Tobago an' de worl'" De leader say, "Yu have money?" Hear Anancy, "Money is no problem, ah have plenty, 'bout ten thousan' dollars!" De leader smile like ah Alligator, an' he say, "Gimme de pan, ah go' give yu ah special!"

Anancy hand over de pan like was ah egg an' he fraid it break. De Leader take it from Anancy, an' start to tune it wit' some serious big cuff . . If yu see him. Do . . cuff, re . . cuff, me . . cuff, cuff . . cuff, fa . . cuff, so . .cuff, cuff, cuff,

cuff, la . . cuff, te . . cuff, cuff, doh . . cuff, cuff, cuff, cuff . . . cuff. In no time at all de pan tune sweet like syrup. Anancy eye get bright when he hear de sweet notes. Den de Guava Stick Satans leader give back Anancy de pan, an' he say, "Yu pan well tune, where de money?"

Now Anancy was so involve in gettin' de pan tune, dat he had forget all about payment. Anancy brains start to tick over like ah ole Mercedes Benz. He decide to try an' confuffle the Leader brains wit' ole talk an' logic. If yu hear him, "Well, yu see, when ah say ah had de money, wha' ah really mean was dat ah judge in de Savannah holdin' it for me, because ah bound to win. So, yu see, in actuality, de money really mine, ah jus' eh collect it yet. But soon as ah get it, which is right after de competition, your money sure!"

Anancy should ah known better. Tryin' to reason with a Guava Stick Satan, is like tryin' to reason wit' ah big stone. De Guava Stick Satans' leader start to change colour one time, fus he vex. He start to swell up like ah Craupaud, an' he shout out for de rest ah de band, "Allyu come quick, ah smartman tryin' to teaf we!" Nex' ting 'bout two hundred Guava Stick Satans come out of de bush, with one set ah big stick, an' iron bolt, an' chain link, an' young boulder. One shout out, "Is dat smartman, Anancy, get him!"

When Anancy hear dat, he grab de pan, an' run for he life, if you see speed, Ben Johnson couldn't catch him. De Guava Stick Steelbandmen pick up one set ah stone, an' start to pelt dem behind Anancy. If you see stone goin' down dat hill, was like 'stone rain.' Poor Anancy. All he could ah do was put de pan on top he head, to shelter from dem stone. Stone start to hit de pan ping! pang! pong! pow! podow! So much stone hit de pan, dat by de time Anancy reach de bottom of de hill de whole pan untune.

Anancy get vex, vex, vex. De pan untune an' he dont have time to get it tune again, because de competition was only ah few days off. So Anancy sit down outside Lal shop to tink. He tink, an' he tink, an' he tink. Den he say, "Ah ha, ah have dem!" Anancy get ah bright idea. So he go down de road an' he climb through ah lady name Miss Lezama window, to use she telephone when she wasn't lookin' . . Because Anancy dont like to pay for telephone calls. he always usin' people telephone when dey not lookin'. Nex' ting de people get some big, big bill from all kind ah places like Africa, New Zealand, an' Acapulco, an' dey don't know how dat happen.

Anyway, Anancy pick up Miss Lezama good, good phone, an' he call up Brer Dog, Brer Cat, Brer Corbeau, Brer Fowl-Cock, Brer Goat, an' Brer Donkey. He tell dem meet him by de Savannah, he have ah big surprise for dem. In no time at all, all man-jack reach down by de Savannah to see wha' Anancy have to offer. Because yu know how some people like freeness an' complimentary. Some ah dem so cheap, dey wouldn't even 'spend ah holiday.'

When dey reach, Anancy greet everybody in fine style, an' put everybody to sit down like de Savannah belong to him, an' start to strut 'bout de place like he in deep thought, an' have so much important tings to say, dat he don't quite know how to start. Is Brer Donkey who start him up, because Brer Donkey leggo one long, steups an' say, "Hear, nah, Brer Anancy. But is wha' really goin' on? Yu bring we down here to tell we someting, but up to now yu eh tell we nutten. You turn politician or what? Say wha' yu have to say now, or all ah we gone, yu hear?"

Anancy pause in mid-step, den he spin round like a ballet dancer for dramatic effect, an' he say, "How would allyu like to make plenty, plenty easy money?" All ah dem shout out, "Yes, man, we in dat!" So Anancy continue, he say, "Well it simple. I go' pay allyu two hundred dollars each, if allyu help me win de pan competition nex' week. You see my pan out ah tune, an' ah cant get it tune-up in time, but ah have ah idea. I go' play ah tune call' "BIG STONE FALLING ON A PAN." All allyu have to do, is hide underneath de stage, an' make allyu mout' sound like ah pan, an' I go pretend dat I beatin' de pan. Nobody go notice de difference, an' ah bound to win. Because allyu go soun' like big stone fallin' on ah pan in trut!."

Brer Donkey say, "Two hundred dollars?" Anancy say,

"Yes, man, two hundred dollars, plus ten percent if rain fall an' allyu get wet." When de res' ah dem hear dat, all man get excited, an dey start to hold big discussion among demselves like is Summit Conference dey havin'. Den dey tell Anancy, "Allright, we go' do it, but we want we money immediately after we done play!" Anancy say, "No problem, dat money in allyu pocket already!"

Well boy, dem animals practice for about ah week, till dey had de whole ting organise properly. Of course Anancy was head an' foot wit' dem, gettin' on as if he study music at de Royal Academy. At last de night of de show reach. Show suppose to start at 8 o'clock, 'bout six o'clock Anancy partners sneak under de Grand-Stand, an' go an' hide under de stage.

In no time at all de stands start to full up wit' people. About thirty thousand people come to see de show. Ten thousand pay, ten thousand get complimentary, an' ten thousand climb over de fence. Later on de promoters say how dey eh make no money, because de ten thousand who pay ask back for dey money. About forty panmen turn up to take part in de competition. Dey was some ah de best panmen in de world, an' dey had some ah de fanciest Tenor Pans yu ever hope to see in yu life, all chrome-up an' shinin', an' tune so fine, dat if yu put yu ears near de pan, yu could hear some notes playin' by deyself.

Well, boy, show start, an' man start to beat pan. Crowd gone wild. About twenty fellas play before Anancy. If you hear sweet pan. Men only beatin' Classics; Tocata an' Fugue, Moonlight Sonata, Waltz of de Flowers. One fella even beat Beethoven Fiftieth Movement. Nobody in de world ever knew dat Beethoven had ah Fiftieth Movement, but dat fella beat it. De crowd give him ah standin' ovation.

Well, boy, time reach for Anancy to play. Anancy walk on stage wit' he out-ah-tune pan. If yu see him. He dress up in scissors-tail coat, ruffle shirt, stripe pants, patent leather shoe, top hat, black bow-tie, an' white gloves. He put in five extra-false-teet to give him a broad smile, so dat de whole Grand Stand could see it, an' he even pay a fella two dollars to blow ah trumpet as he make he entrance. An' dont talk 'bout de 'out-ah-tune pan'. Anancy put so much decorations on it, dat people thought he had invent a new kind ah pan. Most people say it look like ah cross between ah frying pan an' ah satelite. De girls start to whistle, de men get jealous.

Anancy set up he pan right over de spot where he partners hidin' under de stage. He whisper to dem, "Allyu ready?" De partners whisper back, "Yeaaaaaaah!" Den Anancy put on he best Broadcaster voice, like how he does hear dem readin' de news on TTT de TV Station, an' he say, "Ladies and gentlemen, fellow artiste, distinguished guests, it gives me great pleasure to be here tonight participating in this historic pan competition. For my contribution I have chosen an original piece called 'Big Stone Fallin' On A Pan' in G Minor!" De crowd gone wild, dey stamp, dey clap, den dey quiet down.

Anancy pick up de panstick, an' he stamp he foot three times for he partners under de stage to know dat he ready. Den he bow to de audience, lift up de sticks high like he is ah Conductor, den he bend down over de pan an' start to pretend he playin'. As soon as he do dat, he partners under de stage start up wit' dey mout'. Bang, bang, plinket plink, ping, ponky-pong pam pam!" If you hear noise. People never hear nothin' bad so in all dey life.

Dis time if you see Anancy play imaginary pan. He bendin' an' weavin', duckin' he head lef ' an' right, stampin' he foot like he keepin' time, an' he two hand flyin' over de pan like he killin' ants. Meantime under de stage Fowl-Cock crowin', Donkey brayin', Cat meowin', Dog barkin', Goat baaain', an' Corbeau flappin' he wing, keepin' time an' conductin'. All ah dem tryin' to soun' like ah Tenor Pan playin' Big Stone Fallin On A Pan.

After ah time de crowd cant take it no more. Dey start to boo. Nex' ting yu know dey start to pelt all kind ah ting at Anancy — Orange, paper-cup, mango skin, programmes, bite-up hops-bread, an' de people from de South pelt some expensive rolls of toilet paper, dey had flowers on dem. Even de judges throw tings at Anancy, first dem partners sound bad.

Anancy get so vex, he forget all about he partners under de stage. He jus' put de pan over he head, an' he take off like ah jet. All dis time de partners under de stage dont know dat Anancy gone, so dey still playin' pan wit' dey mout', "pang, plilkety, pimm, ding ding, buup." De crowd amaze. Dey hearin' pan, but dey eh have no pan on de stage. Den somebody peep under de stage an' spot de partners.

Well, if you tink dey stone Anancy, yu should see wha' dey do to de partners. Dey pelt everyting dey could find. Ah man even pelt ah bycycle dat ah nuts-vendor was usin' to sell nuts. Dem partners run for dey life. Brer Goat get he head bust. Brer Dog twist he ankle. Brer Fowl-Cock lose half he feathers goin' through de fence. Brer Cat fall in ah pool ah water, an' yu know how cat hate water. Brer Donkey get he ears bend, it take him six weeks to get dem straighten out. Brer Corbeau fly straight into ah Jep nest, an' he get sting all over he bare neck. Someting happen to every one ah dem partners. Dey eh stop runnin' till dey reach ah little way outside Toco, which as yu know, is one ah de furthest parts of Trinidad.

An' who yu tink dey see cock up on ah big stone, drinkin' ah "ice-coconut"? Anancy, of course. Hear Anancy, "But is where you fellas been? Yu know how long I waitin' on allyu? Ah even buy some coconut water for allyu." Anancy lie, Anancy jus' finish teafin' de coconuts off Mr Latchman-Singh tree. Brer Donkey say, "Anancy you an' yu stupidness nearly get us kill. Dis is de last time I goin' in any plan wit' you. Ah dont want no coconut water, jus' give us de two hundred dollars yu promise us, an' we go let bygones be bygones!"

Anancy drop de coconut he was drinkin', he open he eye big, big, like he in shock, an' he bawl out, "Two hundred dollars? Yu mad or wha'? Is allyu make me lose de competition wit' allyu bad singin'. If ah had win de ten thousand dollars ah would ah pay allyu five hundred each, because I is ah generous soul, but ah eh win. So no win, no pay!"

When Brer Donkey hear dat, he get so vex, he spin roun
an' he fire ah back-kick at Anancy. He send Anancy flyin'
through de air like ah football, an' when yu see Anancy hit
de groun', he take off like ah jet, if you see speed. Anancy
run so fast he foot eh touch de gournd yet. Den all de other
animals get vex wit' Brer Donkey. Dey tell him, "If you
didn't kick Anancy so far, we could ah catch him an' get we
money. Now he gone, an' money gone!' An' big argument
break out among dem.

Anancy in de meantime eh stop runnin' till he reach safe
an' sound' where he livin'. An' from dat day to dis, he never
try to enter no steelband competition again.

De moral of de story is, "If you cant do it right dont do
it at all!" Crick. .Crack. . monkey break it back for ah
penny Pommerack!

TANTI MERLE AT PANORAMA

Now Panorama is ah very, very, important part of Carnival.
Yu have Calypso, yu have marse, an' yu have Panorama.
But yu have to know how to go to Panorama, is ah art.
Yu have de North-Stand, yu have de Grand-Stand,
An' yu have de people who don't understand,
But dey all go to Panorama,
Because Panorama is ah very, very important part of Carnival,
Dats where yu have Steelband.
Now I always go to Panorama in de North-Stand,
But before I decide where I really goin',
I does always ask Tanti Merle where she goin',
Because I don't want to go in de same Stand wit' Tanti Merle.
So I ask Tanti Merle if she goin' in de North-Stand,
Well is who tell me do dat! Tanti Merle start up!
She say not she an' no North-Stand,
How de North-Stand is for Vagabonds,
For people who don't have no respect.
Who like to eat food, who like to drink rum, .
Especially if is not dey own.
She say she like to go in de Grand-Stand wit' decent people,

Where she could put down she food an' eat it in peace,
Without no strange people dippin' dey hand in it,
Where only she an' she friends could drink she rum,
An' nobody go come an' pour no kind ah nasty drink
    in she cup,
Tellin' she to "Take ah drink!"
She say she like to go in de Grand-Stand,
Is Hooligans does go in de North-Stand.
Ah say okay Tanti Merle, you go in de Grand-Stand,
I know where I goin', in de North-Stand,
Because I know dat anywhere Tanti Merle go, is trouble.

Now yu have to understan' Panorama in Trinidad.
In de first place, it does take place in ah place call
    de Savannah.
Now in de Savannah at Panorama time dey have someting
    call' 'dust'.
Is ah special kind ah dust yu does only get in Trinidad durin'
    Carnival, is Panorama Dust.
It does start by yu toenail, go up by yu knee,
Reach up by yu waist, go up by yu neck,
An' go down right behind yu nose-hole,
An' stay dey till five months after carnival.
Some people does call it Musical Dust, or Flusian Dust,
Because dat is where all dem foreign flu does hide,
An' have man coughin' for years after Carnival done gone.
When yu go to Panorama an' yu want to find yu friends,
Yu have to do dust like dat, like yu swimming,
Yu does have to clear dust to find dem,
So remember, yu have to watch out for Panorama Dust.
Den de food, Panorama food.
Everybody in Trinidad feel dat at Panorama time
dem turn Chef.
Dey have to cook food to bring to Panorama.
If you see Pelau! Yu hear dem say Carnival is Colour?
Well, when it come to Panorama, Pelau is colour.
Dey have yellow Pelau, green Pelau, orange Pelau, blue Pelau,
It have Pelau wit' no peas, Pelau wit' no 'lau'.

47

Dey even have 'flannel ball Pelau , it look
Like ah tennis ball,
Dey does serve it wit' ah ice-cream scoop,
An' when yu hear dey put it in yu plate,
It fallin' "braps!" an' stand up dey watchin' yu, like dat!
But de more rum yu drink, de nicer de Pelau taste.

But one of de most important parts of Panorama,
Is de Cooler, de Cooler.
Remember, Cooler show status at Panorama,
Depending on how big yu Cooler is, shows how Panoramatic
    you are.
When I first went to Panorama, ah didnt have no friends,
Ah walk wit' ah little flask of rum, an' put it in me
    back-pocket.
De nex' year ah went back, ah had more friends,
Ah walk wit' ah whole bottle ah rum.
De third year ah walk wit' ah bottle an' sandwiches.
The fourth year ah had so many friends,
Ah say ah have to get ah Cooler, ah have status.
So ah go down town to get ah Cooler,
Now remember, at Panorama, Cooler is important.
Ah go through all de shops in town lookin' for Cooler,
Ah find ah Cooler mark 'Igloo'!
Ah say dat have to be ah good Cooler,
Because Igloo belong to dem Esquimoes,
An' dem from up North, so if de Cooler mark Igloo,
It have to be ah good Cooler.
So ah buy me Igloo, ah put me rum in it, me chaser,
Ah put me ice in it, an' ah rest me sandwich on top de ice,
An' ah gone to Panorama.

Now dey have ah set ah people who come to Panorama
Who dont come to hear pan,
As ah matter of fact dey say de pan does disturb de party,
Dey say Panorama would be good if de pan would only
    keep ah little bit quiet,
So dat dey could enjoy deyself.

So ah lot ah dese people go to Panorama to be Panoramatic,
Which mean dey become de pan,
An de pan become ah disturbance to dem.
Now dese people have ah habit of climbin' on people Cooler,
Because dey say dey cant see what goin' on.
Well boy, I bring my good, good Igloo Cooler to Panorama,
But ah did not make allowance for Doreen.
Doreen stand up on my Cooler, say she cannot see pan.
Doreen was not even facin' de stage,
Doreen was watchin' to see who comin' through de
    back gate.
Doreen stand up on my Igloo,
Doreen go right through my Igloo,
My Igloo come like ah Iglee.
Up to now ah have sandwich wit' Doreen footprint on
    it . . . size nine.
This is something Government should go into,
Concrete Cooler.

While all dis goin' on, ah hear big noise in de back of
    de North-Stand.
Ah hear ah voice sayin', "Move! Excuse me please!
Mind yu foot darlin'!"
Now Panorama have about twenty thousand people
Jumpin', wailin', screamin', winin', eatin' dust, catchin' flu,
Excitement goin' on in Panorama,
Somebody sayin', 'Excuse me please, have you no manners,
Can I pass please?, Why aren't you sittin' down?
Let us organise dis crowd!"
Guess who reach in de North-Stand? Tanti Merle! !
Somehow Tanti Merle bounce up ah NCC official,
One ah dose who always feel dem is Prime Minister,
An' does want to show off on ordinary people.
From de time he see Tanti Merle wit' she basket
    by de Grand-Stand,
He say how she is ah vendor, an' she cant go in
    de Grand-Stand,
Because she dont have no accreditation.

NCC have ah ting call accreditation,
Dat mean yu get ah piece ah plastic to put on yu chest,
An' yu could walk all over de place like yu own it,
Only ting is, dey does give it to people
Who only God alone know what dey have to do wit' Carnival.
Well Tanti Merle tell him all about how he mudder make him,
an' all he ancestors,
An' she head for de North-Stand.
An' Tanti Merle bring she Cooler, if yu see Tanti Merle
    Cooler!
It take four men to bring Tanti Merle Cooler in de
    North-Stand.
She get de Cooler from ah Funeral Home.
De Cooler was six foot long an' four foot deep,
It had little curtains round it, wit' ah little glass window
    on top.
An' Tanti Merle showin' manners, because she come in de
    North-Stand, among hooligans.
She say, "Excusssssse me, pleaseeee!"
Well yu know twenty thousand people eh takin' on
    Tanti Merle,
Dey studyin' pan.
Well is now self Tanti Merle get vex,
An' she open she mout' an' she say,
"Ah say Allyu MOVEEEEEEEEE!!!"
Yu ever hear twenty thousand people get quiet?
Twenty thousand people turn round to see who mout' so big.
De place get quiet for about two seconds,
Dat was de first time we hear pan for de day!
When dey see de Cooler comin' through de crowd,
Ah fella say, "O' God, let she pass, somebody dead!"

Well boy, Tanti Merle pass through de crowd, an' she
    settle down,
She move ah set ah chairs, an' she put down de Cooler,
But de Cooler so big, people say how is like she take up ah
    house spot,
An' dey want to know if she have deed.

50

But Tanti Merle eh take dem on, an' everybody settle down
    to watch pan.

An' dat is when de trouble start.

Dey been playin' ah song call' 'Wet Me Down',

An' yu know Trinidadians already,

Dey start to wet down each other wit' Rum, Scotch,
    Soda, anyting.

Ah fella in front throw ah piece ah ice at ah fella in de back,

He miss, an' he hit ah lady call' Miss Piggin.

She was eatin' ah half-dead chicken leg, it had two bite in it,

She get vex an' she pelt it at de fella.

She miss, an' she hit ah fella call Ramlogan,

Who was eating ah real WASA Roti,

It was de most watery Roti I ever see in me life.

Curry was drippin' out it like ah pipe,

Is de only roti I know yu could ah eat wit' ah straw.

Ramlogan get vex an' he pelt de Roti.

He miss! An' guess who he hit? Tanti Merle!

Tanti Merle turn Chinese one time, if you see curry.

Tanti Merle get curry in she eye, she ears, she mout',

All in she hair, down she arms, an' all over she Meiling
    design dress.

Well is who tell Ramlogan do dat!

Tanti Merle get vex, an' nex' ting yu know,

She open up she cooler, push in she hand,

An' she pelt de first ting she pick up.

Ah bowl ah Calaloo soup!

Yu ever see ah bowl ah Calaloo soup fly?

De Calaloo spread out like ah swarm of African Bees!

Tanti Merle wet down 'bout five hundred people one time.

If you see Calaloo, all over people clothes,

Some people look like dey join de army . . green.

Well boy, is den self fight start.

People start peltin' anyting dey had in dey hand,

Which was mostly food an' drink.

Allyu say Trinidad don't have food? Yu jokin'!

Ah fella say call Dr. Commissiong from de Food & Drug
    Commission to put peace.

Dey say was de best fight dey ever had at Panorama,
It take Pan Trinbago 'bout two hours to restore order.
Nex' ting dey cant find Tanti Merle,
Everybody, including de police, lookin' for Tanti Merle.
Dey say dey find she finger print in de Calaloo,
But dey cant find Tanti Merle.
Nex' ting dey hear ah voice bawlin' out.
"Allyu, let me out of hear, allyu deaf or what?"
Guess where Tanti Merle was?
In de Cooler.

VIBERT AND THE PUPPIES

One day Vibert and his friend the "Harrison Boy", who everybody called the "Harrison Boy", but whose real name was George Harrison, were going for a walk. Now Vibert had asked his mother if he could go over by George to play. She said alright, but warned Vibert not to get into any mischief. Because she knew that once he and the "Harrison Boy" got together, things had a habit of happening. Vibert promised faithfully that all they would do is play with the video game that George's big brother had brought for him from America.

So Vibert went over to the "Harrison Boy's" house to play. They played with the new game for about an hour. It was a space game, and they had a lot of fun working the video buttons, and shooting down enemy spaceships that were supposed to be invading Earth. But after a while they began getting bored with being indoors. So they decided to go out into the yard. It was only a matter of time before they found that the yard too, was somehow very boring that morning.

That's when Vibert had a bright idea. He suddenly remembered that Mr. Martin's dog, Kanga, had given birth to some pups the day before. So he said to the "Harrison Boy", "Ah have ah great idea. Let's go an' visit Mr. Martin, an' see de new pups, he tell me ah could come over anytime." The "Harrison Boy" thought for a moment, then said, "Yu sure it go' be okay wit' yu mother? Remember what happen de last

52

time when we went an' see Mrs. Preston body in de Funeral Parlour, without tellin' she? She nearly half-kill yu wit' licks!"

Vibert laughed at the top of his voice, "Nah man, dont worry, she wouldn't even know. We go have time reach by Mr. Martin an' come back, before yu could say 'Mary had ah little lamb'!" So the two of them climbed over the fence, ducked down between the houses so that nobody could see them from Vibert mother's house, and made straight for Mr. Martin's backyard.

When they reached Mr. Martin's backyard, they opened the gate and went inside. It was very quiet. No one was in sight. Vibert called out, "Yoo–hoo, Mr. Martin–o, is me, Vibert!" There was no answer, apparently Mr. Martin had gone out. The "Harrison Boy" looked at Vibert and said, "Is like nobody home. We cant go inside if nobody dey. Mr. Martin not goin' to like it!" Vibert scoffed at him and said, "Nah man, we could go in, Mr. Martin not go' mind, I an' he is personal friend, we used to pitch marble together!" And with that he marched up to the house as if he owned the place, and opened the backdoor which was not locked.

Vibert and the "Harrison Boy" stood for a moment inside the door, then they heard some squealing sounds coming from the kitchen. It was the puppies. They ran over to the kitchen and looked inside. There on the floor beneath the sink were six, beautiful, little puppies, lying on an old sugar bag. They looked like little wobbly balls of fur. Vibert and the "Harrison Boy" were quite excited, and they rushed over to the sink, and began to fuss with the puppies. Laughing and talking at the top of their voices, they picked them up one by one, and began to examine and play with them.

Now everybody knows that you are not supposed to interfere with newborn puppies, especially if their mother is not around. Suddenly there was a snarl from the window. It was Kanga, and she was angry. She wanted to know who was interfering with her pups. . Vibert and the "Harrison Boy" were terrified at the angry face in the window. With a shout of fear, they dropped the puppies they were holding, and ran for their lives . . through the kitchen and out the back door.

With one leap and a snarl, Kanga was through the window and after them. They ran screaming at the top of their voices, with Kanga snapping at their heels, and getting ready to put a mighty bite on the "Harrison Boy" who was lagging behind Vibert. As Kanga opened her jaws to put the bite on the "Harrison Boy's" fat, little behind, a voice shouted out, "Kanga!" It was Mr. Martin. Kanga came to a screeching halt, and Vibert and the "Harrison Boy" flew through the gate, almost trampling Mr. Martin.

Kanga stood in the yard and barked for a while, then forgot all about them, and went back inside to see about her puppies. Vibert and the "Harrison Boy" in the meantime were hanging on to the fence, holding their bellies, and gasping for breath. They looked as if they both had just finished running a marathon. Mr. Martin gave them time to catch their breath, then he said, "Now perhaps you can tell me what that was all about?" Vibert explained, the "Harrison Boy" explained, each one adding on a little more to the story.

At last Mr. Martin said, "It was nice of you to want to come and visit the puppies, but you were wrong to enter the house when you knew that no one was at home. You could have been badly bitten. Mother dogs get very cross with people who interfere with their newborn pups. Even I have to be careful with Kanga and her pups. Let that be a lesson to you. Now run along, and dont let it happen again. We wont tell your mothers this time. But if there is a next time, you will get something worse than a bite from Kanga.

Vibert and the "Harrison Boy" thanked him profusely, and promised never, never to do such a thing again. Then before you could say Kanga they were off down the road, and heading for the safety of their own backyards. They were only about twenty yards from Mr. Martin's house, when Vibert looked over at the "Harrison Boy" and said, "Yu know something? I bet you I could run faster than Kanga. Kanga could ah never catch me!"

VIBERT AND THE HOPS-BREAD

One bright Saturday morning, Vibert and his good friend the "Harrison Boy", decided to go around the neighbourhood to see if they could get some odd-jobs to do. They wanted to make some extra pocket-change to go to matinee. A great western, starring John Wayne, was showing that week. All their friends were going. Vibert and the 'Harrison Boy' had spent most of their pocket-change playing video games in the Mall. So now that Saturday was here, they found that they didn't even have enough money for one of them to go and see the movie.

Sometimes when they were short, or when only one had enough money, then that one would go to see the movie, and on his return, spend the whole time telling the other all about it from start to finish; even who produced and directed. The 'Harrison Boy' used to love to read all the credits on the screen. When everybody else was getting out of their seats as fast as they could, to beat the rush to get out, he would remain in his, reading all the writing on the screen. He never left the cinema until the screen went blank.

As they set off down the road, they worked out a plan of action which they thought could get them the most money with the least effort. Vibert was the chief planner. Somewhere along the way they had picked up an old, empty Condensed Milk tin, and they kicked it along merrily as they walked. Vibert gave it a particularly hard kick which sent it about twenty yards ahead, then he said, "I tink we should split up. You make a pass by Lal Shop an' see if he need help stackin' empty sweet-drink case. If yu eh get nothin' dey, make ah pass by de Barber Shop, dey always need help sweepin' up hair. I go' pass by de restaurant, an' if dat eh wuk, ah go' try de Chinese laundry. Chin does need help hangin' out clothes. Meet me back by Mrs. Padmore house!"

The 'Harrison Boy' agreed, and they parted company, each goin' off in a different direction, but not before Vibert gave the Condensed Milk tin a final kick that sent it sailing into a pile of garbage at the corner of the road.

An hour later Vibert headed for Mrs. Padmore's house. As he approached he saw his friend sitting disconsolately on the curb in front of the house. He was trying to hook a cigarette box out of the drain, with a bent pin on a piece of string. Vibert walked up cheerfully and said, "Is how much yu make?" The 'Harrison Boy' steupsed and said, "Make? Man, those people too cheap. Dey don't want to hire nobody. All dey tellin' me is how dey have enough help already. So I lef' dem wit' dey stupid wuk!"

Vibert plunked himself down besides him on the curb, and said, "Is de same ting wit' me, nobody don't want no help. But ah not sorry, dat restaurant does only have dirty pot to wash, an' is like Chin only washin' dirty sheet dese days. Yu ever hang up ah wet sheet? Not me an' dat!"

They sat together on the curb, thinking on their problem. Vibert watched as the 'Harrison Boy' continued to try to fish the cigarette box out of the drain with the pin and string. Suddenly they both paused. A wonderful smell of baking had, out of the blue, wafted across their noses. They both remembered at the same time. It was Saturday, and that was the day when Mrs. Padmore did her baking.

Mrs. Padmore was one of the best cooks in the whole town, and she ran a little snackette in the downtown area. People came from all over to buy Mrs. Padmore's cakes, bread, pastries and other delicacies. All thought of cinema flew out of Vibert's and the 'Harrison Boy's heads. They both thought 'bread' at the same time.

Vibert watched the 'Harrison Boy' in his eye, and said, "Boy, I could do wit' ah good Hops-Bread right now, what about you?" The 'Harrison Boy' didn't need any encouragement. He rubbed his belly which was always peeping out of his shirt, and said, "Boy, my middle name is Hops-Bread. Let we go an' check it out!"

They dashed across the yard and around to the back of house where the kitchen was. They were just in time to see Mrs. Padmore put a tray full of Hops-Bread on the back window to cool off. It was the most delicious smelling Hops-Bread' you could ever hope to think about. Mrs Padmore had piled them up on the tray, so that they formed something that looked like a small mountain of bread.

The tray was too tempting for Vibert and his partner to pass up. If you hear Vibert, "Let we take one each. It have so much, she not goin' to miss dem. Well, the 'Harrison Boy' didnt like anything better. In two seconds flat they had sneaked over to the side of the house, until they were directly under the window with the tray of hot Hops-Bread.

Vibert who was the leader in this exercise told the 'Harrison Boy', "I go' reach up an' take one, den you reach up an' take one, den we go' take-off. But dont let she see you. As a matter ah fact, de tray right dey, yu dont even have to look, jus' put up yu hand an' ease one out. Dat way she eh go' see yu at all. " The 'Harrison Boy' say, "Is who yu tellin' how to put hand? Yu tink is you alone know how to teaf Hops-Bread?"

By this time they could hear Mrs. Padmore in the room next to the kitchen. Vibert say, "Now is the time!" Slowly he reached up his hand, felt along the window-sill, till he touched the tray. Then reaching up higher, grabbed a hot Hops-Bread off the top of the pile. The Hops-Bread nearly burned his hand. You should see him juggling it from hand to hand to keep from getting his fingers burnt. Then he told the 'Harrison Boy', "Your turn now!"

Following Vibert's expert example, the 'Harrison Boy' reached up slowly, felt along the window-sill till he came to the tray, just as Vibert had done, then he grabbed a hot Hops-Bread. Only one thing, whereas Vibert had grabbed a Hops-Bread from the top of the pile, he grabbed one from the bottom. Yu know what happened next. All the Hops-Bread came tumbling down. If you see bread. On the window, on the floor, on the chair, on the ground, in the yard. As a matter of fact, half the Hops-Bread fell on Vibert and the 'Harrison Boy's' heads. Vibert and the 'Harrison Boy' took off like two jets. Across the yard, over the fence, and down the road. Each one holding a Hops-Bread in his hand.

By this time now Mrs. Padmore had rushed into the kitchen to see what all the noise was about. She let out a scream when she saw all her delicious Hops-Bread scattered all over the floor, and in the yard. And as she looked outside she was just in time to see two little figures jumping over the fence, like it was Olympics. Mrs. Padmore knew those two little figures well, everybody in town knew those two little figures well. In no time at all she was on the phone to Vibert's mother and the 'Harrison Boy's' mother. So by the time they reached home you know what was waiting on them. Licks.

Vibert's mother grabbed him by the collar as he opened the door, and was 'licks like peas'. The neighbours say that all you could hear was Vibert's Mother's voice saying, "Thou shalt not steal!", the sound of a strap, and Vibert bawling for God to come and help him. The same thing was happening to the 'Harrison Boy' on the other side of town. Except the neighbours say that his mother's voice was saying, "Yu shame de whole family!"

To cut a long story short, Vibert and the 'Harrison Boy' got 'ban' from cinema for a month, and all their pocket change had to go to Mrs. Padmore to pay off for the Hops-Bread that had fallen on the ground. Because Mrs. Padmore said how the Hops-Bread got dirty, and she couldn't sell dirty Hops-Bread to her customers. And on top of all that, Vibert and the 'Harrison Boy' had to go and apologise to her. But Mrs. Padmore had a good heart, she cautioned them, and warned them about the police, then she gave each of them a Hops-Bread with cheese. Later on Vibert's mother heard him telling the 'Harrison Boy', "Is ah good ting wasn't soup on dat window!"

DE BEAUTY CONTEST

West Indians love Beauty Contest, ah dont know why. Just say Beauty Contest or Fashion Show, an' place pack up, an' all de ugly people on stage, an' de good-lookin' ones in de audience. But we still love dis ting dey call de Beauty Contest. Now I am ah man who dont believe too much in dis ting dey call de Beauty Contest, because we people so mix up, ah dont know how dey does ever judge beauty in we country. So I dont go by no Beauty Contest unless I wukkin' an' ah gettin' pay. Well boy, one day I dey home, happy, mindin' me business, when dis girl dey call Boopsy turn up on my doorstep, tell me how she want to go up an' enter in ah Beauty Contest. Ah ask her what contest. She say, "De contest name' Miss Compass. Girls from de North, girls from de South, girls from de East an' girls from de West." She want to go up as Miss West. An' she say, "Paul Keens you is ah man always in Theatre, an' on stage, so ah know yu could give me plenty tips to make me win."

Now Boopsy could be ah lot ah tings, Doctor, Lawyer, Engineer, Interior Decorator, all de 'ers', but Beauty Queen, Boopsy cannot make. So ah say, "Boopsy, yu have to get ah sponsor yu know." She say, "But ah have me Sponsor already, man." Ah say, "Who sponsor yuh?" She say, "Ah place call' Eye Sight." Now, Eye Sight is ah establishment dat does make spectacles, glasses, contact lens, shades, an' dem kind ah tings. And I know de Manager have to be blind in one eye, an' cant see in de nex' one, to sponsor Boopsy. Because dey eh call her Boopsy for nothin'. She big so, she big so, she big so, an' she big so, jus' like de Compass she want to go up for. But she tell me dat she goin' up as Miss Eye Sight from de West.

So ah say, "Boopsy, what about de Evening Dress?" She say, "No problem, Tanti Merle designing de Evening Dress." Well, from de time ah hear Tanti Merle name mention, I know ah have to help Boopsy, because de next person to reach on my doorstep in my house, is Tanti Merle, to ask me why.

So ah say alright Boopsy, walk across de room let me see yu walk. Well, is who tell me do dat. Boopsy break me centre table, two side table, she break ah lamp, she mash de cat, almost kill de dog, an' break ah louver in de nex' room. You see, Boopsy have ah basic foot problem. She foot 'Bow' and K at de same time. When Bopsy walkin', is like World Cup yu know, Argentina-Brazil, Argentina-Brazil. Boopsy foot kickin' stone left, right, an' centre.

So ah say, "Boopsy yu have ah foot problem, so ah goin' to train yu to walk like how ah does see dey does train Miss World, an' Miss Universe an' dem kind ah ting." So ah decide to put ah book on she head, an' make her walk like how ah does see dem train models. Well boy, ah try ah Mills An' Boon, ah try ah Prayer Book, ah try ah Dictionary, ah try ah Bible. If you see Boopsy, like ah ship in distress goin' across de room. Is not until ah reach by de Encyclopaedia section dat ah begin to get results. Ah put A,B,C,D,E, by de time ah reach H Boopsy have enough weight on she head, an' she could make it across de room.

Ah say nice, we have dat covered. We train for 'bout six weeks on de walk. Den she tell me how Tanti Merle say she designin' de dress wit' ah bustle in de back to hide she bottom, an' ah ruffle in de front to hide de foot, an' two dart here an' two dart dey, an' in any case she going up as ah Bodybuilder in de Sportswear Category.

So I say if Boopsy do dat she bound to win, because Boopsy look naturally like ah bodybuilder. Because remember dey eh call her Boopsy for nothin', she big so, she big so, she big so, an' she big so.

So ah say, "Boopsy what we have to work on now, is de voice, we have to do some elocution." Because Beauty Queens do not talk, dey elocute. Well, Boopsy problem was volume. . Because Boopsy wukkin' in ah Discoteque, an' she accustom bawlin' out, "Two Rum an' Coke an' ah Juice, quick!" So ah say Boopsy introduce yuself let me hear yu." If you hear Boopsy. She shout out "My name is Boopsyyyyyyyy!" Ah say, "Boopsy not so, not so, tone down, tone down, tone down.". Well, when Boopsy do dat, she look like she goin' an' teaf any minute.

So ah say boy let me let dis girl be natural. So ah say, "Boopsy do what yu want, be natural, walk like de King, wave like de Queen, smile like de Pope, be yuself." She say OK. Ah say nice we have dat covered. An' dat is where trouble does start wit' Trinidadians. After I train Boopsy for 'bout six months, de night before de contest she go by she "friends" for advice. Now it have two set ah people does cause trouble in Trinidad an' Tobago. One set name "Dey". Yu never ever know who 'Dey' are, but yu does always hear. Dey do dis, an' "Dey do dat," an' "Dey against me." De nex' set is "De friends." Yu never ever know who "De friends" are. But yu does always hear how "De friends leading she astray" or "De friends have she dotish." But I didnt know dat. So hear wha' happen.

Well boy, contest night reach. If you see people, because remember was Miss Compass, so people come from all about. People from de North, de South, de East, de West. People from North-North, North-South, North-West. People from all about. Dey come down in dey thousands. An' Tanti Merle come from de West, with about ten thousand people round ah truck. An' she have de dress on de truck, cover down like ah Minshall Marse. An' all de people from de West have big stick, an' boulder, in dey hand. Dem was security for de dress. An' Tanti Merle say nobody could see de dress till she ready, an' it goin' towards de dressin' room like some kind ah Carnival Float.

Well boy, show start. First girl come out, Miss North, she loss on lipstick. Because de judges say, it look as if she put on she lipstick wit' ah broom. She had lipstick all behind she ears, all over she eye-brow. Crowd gone wild. Dey say, "Girl, yu loss. Take she off!" If you hear noise. Next one come up, Miss South. Well, she loss on legs. Because de judges say she legs so thin, she cannot go to England, because she have no visible means of supportin' sheself. Well, crowd gone up, dey gone wild. Noise. Next girl come up, she come up in a stripe-dress. Dey fail her on what dey call misrepresentation.

Because she so thin, de dress only had one stripe on it. So dey say dat could not be ah stripe-dress, because ah stripe-dress must have more dan one stripe. Crowd gone up, dey say. "Boopsy, yu have dem, yu have dem, it in de bag!" De West bias too bad!

Well boy, Boospy turn come, an' Boopsy come out as de Bodybuilder. If you see her. Boopsy start posin' an' showin' muscles. She hit dem ah dis, an' ah dat, an' ah dat, an' ah dat. Crowd gone wild! But what I didnt know was dat Boopsy "friends," de ones she had gone by for advice before de show, had tell her, "Girl, if yu want to win, smile!" Well, Boopsy mout' big, an' it have smile, an' it have smileeeeeeee. Boopsy put down one smile, she frighten all de judges. Boopsy open she mout' so big, you could ah see all she knee-cap. De people from de West gone wild. Dey say, "Oh, smile girl. Boopsy yu have it made, it in de bag!" An' dey start beatin' bottle an' spoon, an' chair, wit' all kind ah ting.

So I send ah message to Boopsy in she dressin' room. Ah say Boopsy be natural, yu smilin' too much. Smile natural. Be a Queen. Wave like de King, walk like de Queen, smile like de Pope, but be yuself, yu understand? be yuself!" Next ting, she Uncle go down an' tell she, how she must not show more dan nine teet when she smile, because if yu show more dan nine teet, dat is indecent exposure.

Boopsy forget me who train she, an' follow she uncle advice. Next appearance on stage, she come up now tryin' to smile only showing nine teet. Boopsy look like ah vaccum cleaner dat vex. Well boy, de crowd didnt care, dey had it, dey went up, dey say, "Oh smile girl, interpretation," Dey say give her marks for creativity, bravery, all kind ah ting. Crowd gone wild. De West bias too bad.

At dis point de MC come an' say, "Ladies and Gentlemen, while de girls go and get ready to make their second appearance in Evening Wear, we shall now bring on de guest artistes." Well de crowd like dat, dey settle down, because you know Trinidad crowd already, guest artistes is like gladiators on de stage, yu does have to fight to survive, dey like to give dem ah hard time if dey eh come up to scratch, peltin' toilet paper an' all kind ah ting.

De first fella come up say he goin' to play Electric Piano — no current. Piano can't start at all. Crowd gettin' restless. De hecklers start up. If yu hear dem. "How yu settin' up so? Yu drink coffee?" "Dat is not ah Piano? Dat is ah dummyno?" So crowd gettin' mad now. De MC say, "Boy, play, forget sound, jus' play, play, play, play!" He play for fifteen minutes, we eh hear nothin' yet. De crowd say, "Nice man, silent night holy night, he good, take him off!"

So dey bring on de nex' guest artiste, a genuine poet from de University of de West Indies. He say, "I shall now do ah love poem straight from de CXC curriculum," an' he start off, "How do I love thee, let me count the ways, one . . . !" People say, "Off man, off de stage, mathematics, off de stage. We dont want no maths here tonight!" Dey start to give him ah hard time.

So dey bring on de Calypsonian, ah fella call de Mighty Mystery. Well was ah mystery how he get on de show. De man cant even talk good, much less sing. Dey boo him before he even start. Dey say he too ugly to sing calypso. Dey boo him, dey boo him, an' he get vex, steups, flip he jacket tail at dem, well cuss dem up, an' walk off de stage. He say he goin' America where people could appreciate he talents.

So dey call out de last guest artiste. Well he wasn't too bad. He say he singing Country & Western, but he choose de wrong song. If yu hear him, he singing "Ah wanna go home!" If yu hear him, "Ah wanna go home, ah wanna go home . . !" People say, "Well go home boy, go home, go home, go home!" Well when de MC realise dat crowd go mash up de show, he say, "The girls will now make their second appearance in their Evening Wear." Crowd quiet down, because dat is what dey come for, queens.

Well boy, de first queen come out. She say, "My dress is called 'Somewhere in Wherever'." People say, "Off man, dat should be somewhere where else!" An' dey start to carry on. Second girl come out, her dress call' "From Here to Extremety." Well boy, bacchanal start, dey say how de dress, too extreme. Den dey say how dey hear is she brudder wearin' de dress, because dey hear she sick in de dressin' room, an' is she brudder wearin' de dress. But nobody could see de girl, so much cloth on de dress, she wrap up from head to foot. But fellas say dey see ah 'man shoes' peepin' out. But up to now nobody know who wear de dress, so was big confusion. Any way, dey say was misrepresentation an' ting, so she pass off.

Next girl come up she say her dress name', "Miss N.A.R!", an' de dress join-up, join-up join-up. Crowd in up-roar, crowd gone up in de air. Dey say politics. Next girl come up her dress name, "I remember COLA", an' de bottom cut-away clean. Boy, crowd gone wild. All de Civil Servants stand up, she get ah standin' ovation, dey say she mus' win it. Next girl come up, her dress call', "De Good De Bad an' de Dhoti." Dey say, "Is ah western dress, take it off, she playin' Indian Cowboy." If you hear dem. Next girl come up now, have on ah tall, tall boots, an' ah short, short dress, an' her dress call', "Puss In Boots." Crowd gone wild. Dey say, "vulgarity, pornography, take it off, off de stage!"

Well boy, Boopsy turn to come on. If you hear de West, de West bias too bad. When dey spot Boopsy, crowd gone up. If you see Boopsy dress. Tanti Merle design ah dress call' "de Pyramid." It start, small, small at de top up here so, an' den it start to spread out, spread out, spread out, like ah waterfall. If you see dress. De West gone wild, dey say, "Girl yu have it, if yu eh get dem on quality yu go get dem on quantity." If you see dress. When Boopsy reach centre stage, dress still comin' out de dressing room. It had fellas wit' stick pushing dress on de stage.

Den Boopsy raise she hand so to show design. If you see sleeve, 'bout fifteen yard of cloth. Den Boopsy bring she hand forward. When she do so, is like Bee Wee now takin' off. Den Boopsy do so, an' bring she hand back for effect, an' she clean off de whole stage. MC, microphone, speakers, musicians, instruments, everyting, gone. Dey still lookin' for two Express reporters, dey cant find dem. As ah matter of fact, dey say how Boopsy take home ah man in she sleeve dat

65

night. Well de West gone wild. Dey say dat dress have it, dat dress have design, it have quality, it have quantity, it have everyting, she must win. Well boy, noise in de place.

Now come de important part, de 'questions' part, dat is where all dem girls does usually fall down. First girl come up, dey ask her, "How much feet in ah yard?" She say, "Well, it depends on how many people in de yard!" Crowd gone up, dey say she loss. Next girl come up, dey ask her, "What is an Indentured Servant?" She say, "An Indentured Servant is ah servant wit' false teet!" Boy, crowd gone up! All de Indians get vex. Dey say she don't know she history. Next girl come up, dey ask her, "Who sponsor Columbus trip round de world!" Hear her, "Neal An' Massy!" Place in uproar. Next girl come up now, dey ask her, "Well if ah white cow gives white milk an' ah black cow gives white milk, what would ah Black & White cow give?" She say, "Black & White milk, nah, what yu expect?" Well boy, crowd say, "Boopsy have it, she beat dem, she must have dis ting, give she, give she, give she!"

Well, Boopsy turn come now, an' Boopsy have to introduce sheself. But I didn't know dat Boopsy "friends" had tell her, "Girl, if yu want to win, use big words." So she come up, an' she stand up so, she take up position number one, like she goin' an' dance ballet, an' she say, "Good evenin' ladies an' gentlemen, my name is Esmerelda Chacon otherwise known as Boopsy. I hails from de Westssssss. (About fifty dog jump de fence.) I represents Miss Eye Sight, makers of glasses, spectacles, contact lens, shades, and other ocular things. (crowd gone wild) I enter this contest because I would like to meet people, preferably boys, big ones. (cheers) I works in a musical establishment which ignorant people does call Discoteque, but it is ah musical establishment. My hobbies are Biology, Psychology, Sociology, Anthropology, Philosophy, Environemntal Control, and other ologies. My ambition is to be an Airhostess an' fly with BeeWee, but if I cant get on to BeeWee I would like to work on a Submarine, because I figures if you cant go up, yu might as well go downnnn!"

Well boy, crowd in uproar. De West gone wild. Dey say

Boopsy have dis ting in de bag, intelligence for so. If you hear dem, de West bias too bad. So time for question now. Boopsy have to pick. Boopsy pick de easiest question in de book, "What is de Capital of Trinidad & Tobago!" Now I didn't know dat Boopsy "friends" had tell her to use big words, but ah find out real quick. Boopsy watch me, she watch ten judges, she watch twenty thousand people, an' she say, "I refuse to answer on de grounds dat it may be taken down and used as evidence against me in a court of law!" Well, boy, crowd gone up. De West gone wild. Dey say, "Give her, give her, give her. Intelligence. Creativity, Bravery. She have it. Give her. We girl win. Intelligence!"

De judges didnt quite know what to do. Dey had conference. Dey put de problem through ah computer. De computer say, "Ask her again!" So dey say, "OK Boopsy, yu have one more chance. Yu have to answer de question to take part in de Contest." Boopsy pick again. Ah nex' easy question. Dey ask her, "What is your favourite dish?" Boopsy watch me, she watch ten judges, she watch twenty thousand people, an' she say, "My favourite dish is Satelite!" Well boy, crowd gone wild, dey jump up on de stage, dey lift up Boopsy in de air, dey wave flag, dey beat pan, dey take over de whole place, dey say, "We girl win it, give her, give her, give her!"

Next ting, results time. De MC start shoutin' out de results. "Third Runner-up, Miss North, (Cheers) Second Runner-up, Miss South, (Cheers) First Runner-up, Miss East er ah sorry, is ah mistake, is Miss West!" Boopsy loss, she come second. Miss East win. Well boy, ah didnt wait to see what happen next, ah run. Ah head for home. Ah jump de fence. Ah leave me car park up in de Savannah, ah get it two days later with four tyres missin'. Ah èh wait for nothin'. Ah head for home, an' ah go under me bed an' hide.

Ah read 'bout it next day in de papers. Three hundred people from de West in Jail. Two judges under emergency operation in de hospital. De promoters in Miami. Dey cant find piece of de Grand Stand, an' de Crown missing. But people say anytime dey go up in de West, an' dey pass by

Boopsy house, dey does see someting shinin' on de piano
.. is de crown.

DONT OPEN YOUR DOOR

(A Christmas Teleplay.)

It's Christmas Eve morning. Carlos, a confirmed bachelor, is
seen in the process of getting up. He glances at the clock.
Looks at the Calendar where Dec. 24th is circled in Red. We
hear his thoughts in a voice over:

Carlos V.O.. . . . . Christmas Eve and not a soul around to
bother my head. (He gets out of bed, goes
to bathroom. Is seen cleaning his teeth etc.
. . voice over continues through all this.)
I could just imagine Zargo an' Boof now,
dey must be up already, catchin' dey tail
cleanin' house an' fixin' up for Father
Christmas. But not your boy, I too smart
for dat. It eh have nothing like ah bachelor
at Christmas Eve. I have 'bout two hundred
places I could eat an' drink, but no hard
work for yours truly. Marriage good for
some people, but not for me. (See him in
kitchen fixing up breakfast) Me fridge well
stock, me place clean, me clothes press, me
gifts all organise, I ready for dem dis
Christmas. De whole day is mine to do as I
please. Imagine Vero tellin' me dat
Christmas is for family an' for children, and
I should get some. Is marriage she anglin'

for, but she have to do better dan dat. I have all de family I need, an' de less I see of dem scamps is de better for me. An' as for children, well, my brothers and sisters have enough for me an' dem. I dont mind children, once I dont have to see dem every day. (He has laid out his breakfast, then goes over to the stereo and puts on some christmas carols) Now dats de spirit of christmas. . food, drink, carols an' peace an' quiet . . . just de atmosphere I need to plan a nice excitin' weekend. Not even Santa Clause could humbug me today. (Sits and starts to eat. Phone rings)

Carlos . . . Is like I talk too soon (Picks up phone, balancing cup in one hand and a bulky looking sandwich in the other) Hello, Buckingham Palace here, Prince Charles speaking . . Ae, ae Zargo is you boy? How yu mean stop playing the fool. Hear nah man, plenty people tell me how I does sound like Prince Charles. Is me face. I have de kind of face dat everybody feel dey see somewhere before. Look, de other day ah little breeze just blow up de little bit of Indian Hair ah have in de front by me forehead, an' if yu hear people . . look at Michael Jackson, look at Michael Jackson. Ha, ha. But is how come yu callin' so early in de mornin' disturbin' dis happy bachelor? Ah married man like you should be burnin' up yu hand boilin' ham instead of disturbin' his Royal Highness (pause) Come an' what? Help you move furniture? Yu have insurance for break back? Where de wife? Oh, she gone by she mother? An' while she helpin' she mother, is me must be helpin' you? No sah, dis is one Christmas

Eve me eh helpin' nobody, yu could vex if yu want, but I have my day plan, an' dat plan dont include moving no furniture. (pause) Monkey say cool breeze? Monkey could say anyting he want, but yu partner not movin'. Ah go see yu, an' dont forget to go to midnight mass. Ha, Ha. (Hangs up) Move furniture, he joking! (Settles back down at table. There is a knock at the door)

Carlos: (Mumbling to himself) Boy ah wonder who knocking my door so early in de mornin'? Couldn't be Vero. Ah hope is not dem people selling books yes, dese blasted people wouldn't give ah man ah chance. (Knock at door. Carlos raises voice) Ah comin', is like yu want to mash it up? (Goes over to door, puts ear to it, and enquires) Who it is?

Neighbour. . . . . . Miss Janice!

Carlos . . . . Miss who?

Neighbour . . . . . . .Ah say Miss Janice. (Carlos looks up to heaven in despair)

Carlos . . . . Is what yu want?

Neighbour . . . . . .Open the door.

Carlos . . . .   Yu can't tell me through de door?

Neighbour . . . . . . Is someting ah want to ask yu, it eh go take long.

Carlos . . . . (opens door reluctantly, sees neighbour) Ah dont have any!

Neighbour . . . . . (pushes past him) Dont have any? Me eh come to borrow nutten!

Carlos . . . . Ah thought was de vaccum cleaner yu did want, like last year.

Neighbour . . . . . . Vaccum Cleaner? Nah man, ah dont need dat till after Boxing Day, ah hope it wukkin'. Ah tell yu yu should ah buy de other brand. My girlfriend have one like yours, an' is endless horrors. (She goes over to table and takes piece of Carlos' toast) But is like yu burn dis toast, ah tell yu yu need ah good wife to take care of you.

Carlos . . . . (annoyed) Ah thought yu said yu had something to ask me? Ah hope is not money yu want borrow, because I flat brokes. I give way my wallet yesterday, it eh servin' no purpose. What is de sense of havin' a wallet an' yu dont have no money.?

Neighbour . . . . . . Is not money I want man, I is ah woman does pay my own way, my mudder always used to tell me 'Neither ah lender or ah borrower be!' Ah want yu to do me ah favour.

Carlos . . . . What is de favour?

Neighbour . . . . . . Ah want yu to come down town wit' me, an' help me pick up ah potted plant!

Carlos . . . . Potted plant? In my good car? Woman yu mad or what?

Neighbour . . . . . . (Pleads) Oh gosh, yu bound to get on so? Is only ah little potted plant me daughter choose out for me as ah gift, an' ah cant get no transport to go an' get it. Is Christmas Eve, an' every place ah call tellin' me how dey busy! You is de only man I know who have transport round here! Help me out, nah?

Carlos . . . . Lady ah fella charge me forty dollars to compound me car, an' it look more like he pound it instead of compound it. He mash up de outside, now you want to finish off de inside? Is no way I putting no potted plant in my good car. Plus yu know how much traffic it must be have downtown all now so? Ah wouldnt be

71

surprise if Santa Clause an' he reindeer get stick in traffic. Leave de plant till after Christmas, an' ah go pick it up for you wit' me cousin truck!

Neighbour . . . . . (switches to tears) Yu mean to say yu go really do me dat? Where is yu Christmas spirit? What it go take out ah yu to put ah little potted plant in yu car? Tink how me daughter go feel when she look under de tree Christmas morning, an' she dont see de plant she choose for she one an' only mudder? De Lord go bless yu forever if yu do ah good deed on Christmas Eve. Yu eh doing nutten here but eatin' burn toast, help out yu neighbour, nah?

Carlos . . . . An' wha' 'bout de gas for me car? Yu tink it easy to drive car in Trinidad dese days? Gas gone up so high I could only afford de fumes. Is recession yu know, everyting cost money. We go spend twenty dollars in gas to pick up ah five dollar potted plant!

Neighbour . . . . . Alright, ah go put de gas.

Carlos . . . . Me shocks bad too.

Neighbour . . . . . . Wait, nah, is ah new car yu want? Shocks? Why yu dont ask for ah paint job too? Yu surprise me man, yu shocks me. Ah wasnt lookin' for yu dey at all. Tell me straight if yu go help me out, let me go my way before ah Christmas blight take me in dis house.

Carlos . . . . Alright, ah go help yu out. But ah warnin' yu, if dat potted plant nasty my car, Christmas or no Christmas, is outside it going.

Neighbour . . . . . . (All smiles) God go bless yu. Ah sure if yu mother was here she would be proud ah yu. Dont worry man, it eh go be no

	problem, wait an' see. It go fit cool, cool, an' besides, ah go spread paper on de ground, so it eh go nasty-up yu car.
Carlos	Ok. Ok, but do fast, if we goin' we have to go now before traffic start to hot up. Give me five minutes to finish me breakfast, den meet me by de gate. Dont let me wait, yu know, ah not skylarkin' dis Christmas Eve mornin'.
Neighbour	Nah man, I ready as Freddy. (goes to door). If I was you ah would scrape dat toast before ah eat it. (Exits)
Carlos	(In exasperation) Why me Lord, why me? Mih whole day spoil! (Fade Out.)

SCENE II

Neighbour and Carlos are seen in car heading for Port of Spain. Cameras are to take in a panoramic view of the city highlights, and all the hustle and bustle of Christmas. The car is blocked by a madman in dirty pants, no shirt and no shoes, as is often seen on the streets of Port of Spain. He is walking in circles in front of the car. (Christmas music in background)

Neighbour	Aye you, get yu tail out de road before ah knock yu down.
Carlos	Leave de man, yu hear. Next ting yu know he throw some bottle through me windscreen.
Neighbour	Is ah disgrace man, ah dont know why de government dont lock up dem mad people. (To madman) Aye yu, move yu mad self out de road. (To Carlos) Blow yu horn. (Carlos blows horn) (Madman stops and gives them a circular blessing, shakes his bottom at them, and moves on)
Neighbour	Well I never see more. Imagine ah respectable woman like me have to put up with dis sort of behaviour.

73

Carlos . . . . Is not you vote for de government last year? It serve allyu right, dey should leggo all de mad people in de madhouse, because dey eh more mad dan de people who runnin' dis country.

(Car proceeds then is blocked again, this time by a Taxi driver having a conversation with a pedestrian in the middle of the road)

Carlos . . . . (Blows horn) Yu see why I doesn't want to leave my house when mornin' come? Look at ignorance. (Blows horn. . Taxi-driver ignores him)

Neighbour . . . . . (pushes head out window) Excuse me, yu mind moving yu car so we could pass? (Taxi ignores her) Dats why government should put more bus in allyu tail, allyu should starve. (She is halfway out the window) If ah had half a nose ah wouldnt want to be ah taxi-driver.

Pedestrian . .. . . . So what happen, you is ah Russian? Yu cant see we having ah conversation going on?

Neighbour . . . . . O' God we on ah mission. Have some consideration nah, allyu tink allyu own de blasted road. (As she is talking a small pickup truck with a Parang group drives up playing music. It tries to inch past the taxi and gets stuck. Nobody is interested in moving now, as everybody gathers round the traffic jam to listen to the music. At last Carlos and the neighbour get through, and we see them driving off then arriving in front of a department store. After much twisting and turning, Carlos manages to park the car, with plenty directions from neighbour who comes out of car to assist)

Carlos . . . . Lord, me whole day spoil. (To Neighbour)

74

OK let us go an' get yu potted plant, yu hear, so ah could get back to de peace an' quiet of me house. (Raises eyes to heaven, camera shows store sign saying 'We wish you a Merry Christmas) Lord, why Me?

SCENE III   Inside Store

Carlos and Neighbour are seen going up Escalator inside store. Camera focuses on Christmas decorations etc. They arrive at the potted plants section. They look over the variety of plants. Carlos is looking at the small, cute plants.

Carlos . . . . .Ae, ae dese don't look too bad. Dat one over dey must be de one yu daughter put aside for yu. Look, it mark 'sold'. Yu know it mightnt be ah bad idea for me to pick up ah few for me apartment, could brighten up de place.

Neighbour . . . . . .You would starve dem plants to death. Yu need ah wife to take care of dem kind ah ting.

Carlos . . . . .You dont tell me what I need, just go an find out which ah dese plants belong to you, so we could leave dis place.

Neighbour . . . . . .(Goes up to department manager who has been eyeing them suspiciously. He is a very prim and proper type, who loves to use big words to impress people) Excuse me sah, but ah tryin' to find out where ah could pick up ah potted plant me daughter leave here for me. De name is Veronica Simmons.

Manager . . . . I dear say that shouldnt be a problem at all, just one moment please. (exits)

Carlos . . . . .Dey must be have yours in ah special place. I thought was one ah dese over here. Ah hope yu daughter pay for it already, because me eh have no money to rescue no potted plant.

	(Manager returns carrying a seven foot Christmas Tree)
Manager	Here is your article madam.
Carlos	(In shock) Potted plant? Dat is ah potted plant? Dat eh no potted plant. Dat is ah Christmas Tree, an' no way in dis life or de nex', dat goin' in or on my expensive motocar.
Neighbour	Is not my fault. De girl tell me potted plant, she never tell me Christmas Tree. Yu tink ah dont know de difference between ah potted plant an' ah Christmas Tree? To hear yu talk yu would tink dat de tree is some kinda beast or something. Is just ah tree, how it go nasty yu stupid motocar?
Carlos	So now my car stupid? Yu see what ah mean, Lord! Ah tell yu from we leave home dat ah not nastyin' up me car. Ah tell yu in English an' dialect. An' in any case dat tree can't fit inside my car, so is where it goin'?
Neighbour	So is what yu sayin'? Ah must throw way me expensive tree? (Starts to cry) De one tree me only daughter buy for she only mother? Allyu too wicked.
	(Shoppers attracted by the argument start to gather round the three of them.)
Manager	Pray tell, what seems to be the problem? Maybe I can be of some general assistance. (Everybody starts to talk at the same time, including members of the crowd which by now is quite thick)
Manager	(holding up his hands for silence) Momentarily, momentarily. Verily we cannot all converse at the same time. Having assessed your situation, it seems to me that you have a problem of structural size. The obvious answer to your predicament, there-

fore, is to shorten the length of the article so that it can fit more comfortably into your vehicle. (Bends down behind counter and comes up with a shiny cutlass.) And I have just the thing to do it right here. Why dont you cut off these two bottom branches. (He cuts off two branches. The tree gets shorter)

Neighbour . . . . . (Looking critically at tree) Ah find it lookin' too lopsided, cut off two more by here so. (She points. Manager cuts off two more. Tree gets shorter. Crowd is looking on excitedly. A little boy in the crowd shouts out!)

Little Boy. . . . . . Dem two in de bottom dey look like dey rotten, cut dem off. (Manager cuts off two more branches. Tree gets shorter)

Neighbour . . . . . (Looks at tree which is now very short and burst into tears) De tree too short, allyu cut off too much. Ah tell allyu not to cut off too much. (To manager) Is your fault, yu cut up me tree, now it spoil for good.

Manager . . . . (Very haughtily) Madam it was at your request that I cut this tree. It is you who wanted this arboreal delight crammed into some mingy vehicle.

Carlos . . . . .Watch who car yu callin' mingy, yu better ketch yuself. Yu know how much ah car like dat cost? Mingy? Ah go show yu mingy!

Neighbour . . . . . .Is he fault. Is my tree, but is he who bring de cutlass to shorten de tree. Not so? (Appeals to the crowd)

Voices from
crowd . . . . De woman right? Dis store have plenty money! Give she ah new tree. (Begin to chant waving the cut off branches) New Tree, New Tree, New Tree!!!!

Carlos . . . .(Draws manager aside) Hear nah man, allyu have any ah dem artificial tree inside?

Manager . . . . But of course, this establishment stocks all kinds of stocks. When it comes to stocks, we got the stocks. (He hurries away through chanting crowd. The parang group has now arrived, and joins in the general confusion singing "New Tree" in Parang style. Manager returns with box with Christmas Tree, opens it in middle of crowd.)

Manager . . . . Madam on behalf of this establishment and in the true spirit of the Christmas season, it gives me great pleasure to present you with this Tree. (The crowd cheers, Carlos picks up box and heads out the store, leading Parang group etc. singing. Camera close up on Carlos)

Carlos . . . . .Lord, me whole day spoil. Is who tell me to open mih door?

(All exit down escalator. Last shot of Box on Carlos head in the midst of crowd, people still waving cut-off branches.)

The End.

DE RAT TALE

(A narrative description written as commentary for the 1986 Carnival band Rat Race, designed and produced by Peter Minshall. Story was read live as band crossed the Savannah stage.)

Once long ago, before your time, before my time, before anybody time, de Great Cat in de sky drop two piece ah cheese in de Caribbean Sea. For years de two piece ah cheese float in de sea, an' dey grow an swell wit' de salt water. An' in no time at all dey was two ah de most beautiful piece ah cheese you could ever hope to see in yu life. An' de Great Cat was happy, because dey was meant for de benefit of man, to make man happy. But man was too greedy.

One day some Ciboney Indians see de cheese, an' dey say, "Chee wees, dat is cheese!" An' dey jump on de cheese, an' dey start to nibble, nibble de cheese, like is dat dey born to do, an' dey call de cheese 'Ciboney Cheese'.

Nex' ting yu know, ah set ah Indian call' Carib hear 'bout de Ciboney an' dey cheese. An' dey get cheesed off wit' de Ciboney an' dem, because dey say how dey too selfish, an' is like dey want all de cheese for deyself. An' dey say how de Ciboney should share de cheese de Carib way, which is 'all for me an' none for you!' So when de Ciboney tell dem 'Chee Wees!", dey say, "Chee wees? Is we cheese!" An' in no time at all dem Carib 'share out' de Ciboney, an' was 'Carib Cheese' down de line. But dem Carib didn't jus' nibble, nibble, nibble, dey start to 'bite bite'!

While all dis goin' on, what yu tink happen? Two set ah folks arrive on de scene. One call deyself de Spanish, de other call deyself de French. Dey didnt like each other much, but one ting de both ah dem like, was cheese. An' in no time at all dey chase way de Caribs, an' was fight down de line for Cheese. De Spanish only shoutin' out, "Hello Amigo!" an' all dis time dey stuffin' dey mout' wit' cheese. De French mean time only complainin' how, "Zee French are zee best cooks, is we know 'bout zee cheese an' zem, so is we who should own zis cheese!" An' is so dey carryin' on wit' gun an' cannon, one sayin' is 'Spanish Cheese', de other sayin' how is 'French Cheese',

Dey make so much noise dat you could ah hear dem quite up in ah place call' England. So who yu tink reach nex'? De Englishman of course. If you hear him, "I say what ole chap, those Frenchies and Amigos are wasting that cheese. Let's take it over and show those blokes how it is done!" An' yu know, to do it de English way, is to get some-body else to do it for yu. Especially as to how dey didn't want jus' piece ah de cheese, dey wanted de whole ting. But was ah cheesy situation, because de Cheese was too much for de Englishman to handle by deyself. So dey chase off de French an' de Spanish, take over de cheese, den go quite in Africa an' India, an' drag down one set ah Black people an' Indian, to help dem cut up de cheese, so dat dey could eat it up better. Dey didnt want to nibble nibble, or bite bite, or stuff stuff, dey wanted to 'dine'.

But as de years pass, de workers get vex, because dey only workin' in cheese but dey cant get no cheese. . Till one day dey tell de Englishman, "We wukkin' cheese, so we takin' cheese!" By dis time de Englishman was fed up wit' cheese, because he had try to do too much wit' de cheese. Dey had Cheese-cake, Cheese-dip, Bread an' Cheese, Cheese-Puff, Guave Cheese, all kinda cheese ting. Dey even had Cheese Cloth. So he say "Okay, allyu want cheese? Take Cheese!"

An' dat is when de bacchanal start. Because de workers was waitin' so long to get de cheese, dat when dey get it dey couldn't decide how to share it. In no time at all, it was all man for deyself. Who vex . . vex, who vex . . loss. An' dat is when de rats decide to make dey move an' take over de cheese. Because dey realise dat de people didn't just want to nibble nibble, or bite bite, or stuff, stuff, or dine dine, dey wanted to "nyam!" De rats say, "Dese ordinary people dont know how to appreciate good cheese. Dey go waste it. Dey need us to tell dem how to handle cheese; after all we is rats, an' yu know rat an' cheese go together like ham an' hops. Let we invade an' take over, before dey do someting stupid like give cheese to every Tom, Wong, Aziz, Harrylal, an' Wantumi." So dey invade.

De first set to attack was de Desert Rats. If yu see dem firin' gun like dey mad, an' crawlin' on dey belly, an' rollin' on de groun' like Audie Murphy in 'To Hell an' Back!' Yu ever hear 'bout Soldier Crab? Well, dese was Soldier Rat. Desert Rat could eat you for lunch an' desert, first dey bad. Ah lot ah dem study war in de cinema under John Wayne. Dey train wit' movies like Back to Bataan, De Halls Of Montezuma, an' Fort Apache. Ah tell yu, de Desert Rats was someting else. Yu ever hear 'bout de Dirty Dozen?

Well in dis case was "De Dirty Thousan'" Is ah good ting dey didnt have Nuclear Weapon, otherwise all now so cheese melt.

Well when de more intelligent rats see wha' was goin' on, dey realise dat tings might get worse before dey get better, an' dat de cheese definitely wasn't wort' gettin' kill for. So dey decide to abandon ship. Talk 'bout rats leavin' ah sinkin' ship? If you see rats bail out. Dey must ah hear Gypsy calypso. Yu ever see tourists comin' off ah ship to visit de island? Well dat was joke compare to how dese rats abandon ship. Some leave in car, in bus, in train. Some take plane, some take jet, some take taxi. Some leave wit' suitcase, paper bag, trunk. Some jus' leave wit' dey bankbook. Was ah straight case of 'ship sinkin' rat leavin'. Some sell dey house, dey land, dey apartment. Some laugh, some cry, some couldn't care less. Was Rats leaving de sinking ship.

Den some ah de rats dat remain decide dat dey should take over other things besides de cheese, so dat dey could have more an' bigger territory. So dey decide to invade ah place call Balisier. Now as yu know, Balisier is de place where Snake does live. So when Snake see de rats comin', he say, "But wha' goin' on? Dey have plenty room in dis Balisier for everybody to live peacefully. Plus it have plenty cheese!" De rats say, "Cheese? Take cheese in yu tail!" An' was blows! Snake had to run for he life. Was rats all over Balisier. Dey take over upstairs, downstairs, kitchen an' coop. Dey take over inside, outside, an' backside. De Balisier turn 'bazoody' wit' rats, an' dey start callin' it Ratisier!

Den ah set ah rats decide dat dem rats dat chase way de Snakes look like dey plan to takeover not only de Balisier, but everyting else in sight. So dey decide dat before dey get eraticated, dey should do someting fast. So dey form someting call' de National Alliance of Rats. Was ah whole mix-up of different kinds ah rats. Dey had Cane-rats, Oil-rats, Democ-rats, an' Labour-rats. Dey had some who were Moderat an' some who were not so Moderat, an' dey defininitely had plenty Raticals. Most of dem didn't even like each other, an' was always fightin' an' carryin' on. But dey stayed together, because basically dey were all Politirats.

Well while all dis fightin' an' takin' over was goin' on ah nex' set ah rats was tryin' to keep de cheese from fermentin' an' gettin' stale. Dey was also tryin' to control de cheese in ah smart way. So dey start to pass all kind ah laws an' ting, so dat people couldn't get away wit' too much cheese. Everybody call dese rats de Beureauc-rats. Yu know how yu mother beureau does have plenty drawers? Well de Beureauc-rats try to put everybody in ah different drawer, like little boxes, so dat dey couldn't come out unless somebody let dem out. An' jus' to make sure dat nobody eh come out from where dey put dem, de Beureauc-rats tie up everybody wit' Red Tape.

All where yu go yu gettin' tie up wit' Red Tape. Was de most popular tape in town. When yu hear somebody tie you up wit' Red Tape, yu well tie. Was endless confusion, because after ah time even de Beureauc-rats get tie up wit' Red Tape.

Well de Red Tape get some rats so frustrated dat dey start to "go off", an' when ah say "go off", ah don't mean on holiday. Ah mean dey begin to get 'mental'. Dey didn't know what nex' to do wit' demselves. Dey start to experiment wit' life. Dey get tired wit' Scotch, an' Rum, an' Wine, an' Sherry, an' Brandy. Dey start takin' Rat Poison.

Now is not every poison look like poison, an' taste like poison, so dat ah lot ah dem thought dat Rat Poison was ah great ting. Dey had poison in all shape an' form, an' by all different name. But de dreadest poison of dem all was de White Poison, de Powder. De White Poison had rats goin' mad. Runnin', jumpin', shootin', rapin'. It had some feelin' like Superstars. It had some feelin' like Super Dead. An' it had some dat were definitely dead, dead, dead. Yu ever smell ah dead rat?

But de poison wasn't only in de belly an' de blood, it was in de mind too. An' suddenly some rats begin to look at each other in ah different way, an' begin to say how dis rat better dan dat rat, an' how dat rat better dan dis rat. Dey forget dat dey was all fightin' for de same cheese, an' dey come out to kill each other, all because some was different to others. If you see dem, Black Rats, Brown Rats, Pink Rats, White Rats, Yellow Rats. Light-Black, Black-Black, Blue-Black, Light Brown. Rats wit' straight hair, rats wit' curly hair, rats wit' afro, rats wit' gerry-curl. Rats wit' no hair. Even rats wit' wigs. De Race Rats start to mash up de cheese.

Tings get so bad dat rats begin to attack dey own family. Everybody start to bawl out Fratricide. Was father against son, son against father. Mother against daughter, daughter against mother. Cousin against cousin, sister against sister, brother against brother. Even 'outside chile' against inside chile. Was Fratricide down de line.

As de rats continue to fight among demselves, de situation became 'ratid'! You could find de fightin' everywhere, even among de pigeons. An' when yu find rats among de pigeons, yu know wha' dat mean, is de innocent payin' for de guilty, is rats gettin' eratic. But even while all dis was goin' on, some rats were havin' ah good time. Dey didnt care 'bout de rest ah de rats, or who was killin' who, because dey thought dat dey was de 'cats whiskers.' Dey was only enterested in dressin' up in pretty clothes, an' galleryin' deyselves. Dese were de 'Pretty Rats.'

You could always spot dem, because dey was always dressed up in frivolous, jivolous, glitter an' glatter. Dey rushed all over de cheese. Yu could find dem on de islands in de sun, in de fiestas, wearin' sombreros, an' carryin' on at ah rate playin' demselves. An' when yu hear dey get together, was ah straight case of Ratorama. An' while dey was havin' ah pretty good time, de cheese was smellin' pretty bad. De pretty rats didn't want to listen or hear. Dey wanted to forget dat dey too were jus' like all de other greedy rats.

In de meantime, de rats in de Market Place was takin' over all de extra food, jus' in case de cheese run out. Dey decide to control de land through de food. Because dey figure de cheese had to done sometime, an' land dont spoil, an' who control de land control de food, an' who control de food control de land. So de first place dey try to take over was de markets wit' all de food.

So was rats in every market in de land. Was rats in de town market, rats in de country market, rats in de Caricom Market, rats in de Common Market. Nex' ting yu know was rats in de Caribbean Basin. Dey leave market an' jump in basin, but dey was still takin' basket. De biggest rats however, forget bout de local markets. Dey take over de Stock Markets an' start to hand out 'shares'.

But was de little rats I feel sorry for. Dey had to struggle to grow up in all de bacchanal of de rats 'take over'! Dey had to fight to get education, an' dey became Common Entrats, fighting to get into schools all over de land whether dey learn anyting or not. Dey had one thousan' seats an' ten thousan' Common Entrats, so yu know was jammin' down de line. In no time at all de Common Entrats became a mass of Brats, fightin' each other for seats dat did not exist. An' when dey get in de school was another story, no Teacherats.

Meantime de Mauvais Langue rats was bad-talkin' people all over de place. Dey was rats wit' sharp tongues, an' dey specialise in rumours an' rumour of rumours. Dey was killin' people lef ', right, an' centre wit' character assasination an' blackmail. Dey was anywhere dey could get ah chance to bad-talk people. On de radio, in de Press, at de University, on de TV, in de political meetings, in de bookshops, in de Art Galleries, in de church. Some call demselves Editors, some call demselves critics, some even had dey PhD. Dey was everywhere, an' dey favourite warcry was, "Allyu eh hear?" Was ah "he say", an' ah "she say", an' ah "dem say." Was mauvais langue down de line. Was rats rattin' on rats.

All dis time de High Fashion Rats couldn't care less, dey was only enterested in fashion, misleadin' people wit' all kind ah style dat nobody could wear, an' havin' people dislikin' demselves because dey couldn't look like somebody else. An' was straight copy of de foreign styles. Yu ever hear 'bout Copycat? Well dey had Copyrat. Dey had high fashion an' low fashion. Fashion from England, fashion from France. Fashion from America an' fashion from Italy. Yu ever hear how "follow fashion kill Miss Ison big Bull Dog?" Well follow-fashion kill plenty rats.

Ah close friend of de High Fashion Rats was de Aristoc-Rats. Dey had de money to buy de high fashion, an' dey thought dat dey was better dan everybody else, because dey was Aristoc-Rats. If you see dem drivin' 'bout an' talkin' in big voices, an' dressin' up in de latest fashion, an buyin' de best of everyting. But dey forget dat under it all, dey was jus' rats like everybody else, especially those who had gone from rats to riches.

Meantime de Worker Rats who had take over de cheese in de first place, was catchin' dey tail to survive. Dey found dat dey was still workin' for other rats, an' dat dey still wasnt gettin' enough cheese. An' dey begin to feel dat dey was better off when dey used to work for de Englishman. So de Worker Rats begin to form tings call Unions, an' have strikes, an' demonstrate, an' demand de same cheese dat dey had demand in de beginnin' of de story.

An' while everybody was fightin' to survive an' control de cheese, nobody was takin' care of de cheese. An' it begin to ferment, an' get mouldy, an' run-down, an' soon many rats couldn't remember why dey was fightin', an' what had start de whole bacchanal in de first place. Everybody was runnin' madly along, in ah race towards nobody knew where. It was de Rat Race to Extinction!

It seemed like dere was no turnin' back. Hundreds of rats just collapse' an' dead. Others just wandered aimlessly, till dey too pass away. Until de only ones left was de Vagrats, all torn an' tattered, askin' demselves, why? An' even dey too pass away, wit' ah groan an' ah rattle, an' ah backward glance at what might have been. An' de cheese stan' still.

An' so de story end. Is it ah Rat Tale? Or is it de tale of man? I dont know, I only tellin' you what dey tell me. Wire bend, story end, Crick Crack!!

AH DONKEY CALL' BASCOMBE

A donkey call' Bascombe kick a motorcar,
It happen up in Arima.
The donkey get vex with Mr. Bubb,
The fella who was the owner.
You see Mr. Bubb was a farmer,
And he had a donkey cart,
Then he decide to buy a Mazda,
And thats when the trouble start.
Bascombe didnt like the Mazda,
He thought it would replace he,
From what they make me to understand,
Was a straight case of jealousy.

(CHORUS)
Bascombe get vex, vex, vex,
An' he kick up the motorcar
Bascombe get vex, vex, vex,
An' he only bawling he-haw.
He mash up de fender,
He dent up de bumper,
People get in a fright,
With one swing of he back-foot,
Bascombe out de Motorcar light.

When Mr. Bubb see the situation,
He try to pacify Bascombe,
He give him some grass,
Two bucket of water,
And a holiday out in the pasture.
He even put mag-rims on the Donkey-cart wheel,
To show Bascombe just how he feel,
But as soon as he go to start up the Mazda
Well that was another matter.

(CHORUS)
At last Mr. Bubb organise a plan,
To get on the good side of Bascombe,
Once every week he tie the cart to the car,

And call it a Donkey-Cart-Mazda.
Bascombe now feeling real happy,
Anytime they drive in the country,
For it was the only motor-car,
That had a man-chauffeur,
And a donkey for passenger.

CARNIVAL IS MARSE

Yu know, plenty people like to feel dat because yu come from Trinidad, yu suppose to be able to dance, yu suppose to like Pelau an' dem kind ah ting, an' yu suppose to like Calypso an' be able to sing it too. Dey cant understand when ah man say he don't play Carnival. "Someting got to be wrong wit' he, he not from here, where he come from?" But yu see, some people born to play, an' some people born to 'spectate', to look on.

Well I tink I am ah born spectator, because I not lucky wit' carnival band at all, at all. I have ah history of bad luck wit' carnival band. De first band I ever play wit' in my life, was ah band call' "De Horrors of Dracula." Well, was real horrors. Was ah 'Small Band,' ah real small, band, ah mean de band was so small, de whole side went to de Savannah in ah taxi. Dat was ah 'small band.' If you see us dress-up like dis Dracula, one set ah black clothes, an' cape all down to de ground. An' if you see false teet' in we mout.' One Dr. Watts make de false teet for we. Man only keep bitin' deyself. When we cross de stage, nobody was quite sure what we was. Our band was de only band ever win 'Individual Of De Year.'

An' we put on big act yu know. I had on ah raincoat over me costume, an' de rest of de band was suppose to surround me on stage like dey bitin' me, an' I had was to take off de raincoat, an' come out in me costume like I turn ah Dracula. An' ah fella was suppose to drop some ole bones on de ground to represent my body. Only problem was, he couldn't get no human bones; so he gone by de butcher an' get some ole cow head, an' pig foot, an' sheep ribs, an' tings like dat, an' is dat de man put on de stage. Well, yu could imagine laugh. If dey had ah comedy prize we would ah sure win dat. After dat, ah tell dem not me an' Carnival, ah say it must have more to Carnival dan dat.

De nex' year dey come an' tell me how de mistake ah make was goin' an' play in ah Small Band. Dey say, "Boy, yu play de wrong ting, join ah Medium Size Band, Small Band is for little boys, Medium Size Band is for big man!" Den dey tell me how dey playin' something call' "De Glories Dat Was Greece." Dey tell me how I goin' to be ah Roman Emperor, den dey tell me ah should try for someting ah little bigger, so I end up as "Mars — The God Of War."

Well, de costume wasn't too bad, but de problem was de helmet. Yu see in those days, yu didnt buy nothin', yu had to make it yuself. An' if you wasnt too artistic, an' couldnt make yu own helmet, yu had to get somebody to make it for yu. Well, de fella who make my helmet was either Cokey-eye, or else he was blind in one eye an' can't see in de next one. If you see de helmet. De front like it vex wit' de back. De front gone so, an' de back gone so. When ah put it on, ah look as if ah have ah bolt of lightning on top me head. Ah had headache for 'bout ten years after dat. Ah say it must have more to Carnival dan dat.

Den one day ah fella come an' tell me, "Forget dem amateurs, if yu want to play real mas', play wit' ah professional." He tell me play wit' Saldenah, dat is ah real Mas'-man! So poor me go an' sign up wit' Sally. Dat year Sally play "Ah Sailor Is Ah Sailor" — I was ah 'Drunken Sailor'. De only section ah could get in. Ah eh know nobody in de section. Yu ever play in ah section an' yu eh know nobody in it? Den dey tell me how my section comin' out from Diego-Martin, to go down dey early Carnival Monday mornin' an collect me costume.

So I gone down dey Carnival Monday mornin'. When ah ask for me costume, ah lil skinny fella tell me wait, an' he gone in de back. Well he gone so long, ah say dey mus' be now sewin' it. Nex' ting ah see ah fella comin' wit' someting dat look like ah Engagement Ring box. My costume was in dat. Five hundred dollars wort' of costume, in ah Engagement Ring box.

An' if you see costume. De fella who shop for Sally, like he buy everyting de same size. Ah had purple bell-bottom pants. If you see dem. Three foot in front, three foot behind. When ah do so, me foot lookin' like ah axe. Like de man who buy for Sally really didnt know nothin' 'bout size in trut.' We had ah white tank-top vest 'bout five size too small. When ah put it on, it cant go inside me pants at all, at all. So ah had to bend over, push it in me waist, an' stay so for de whole day. If ah ever do so, tank-top flyin' up an' hit me in me nose.

As for de hat an' dem, well he buy all hat de same size, size three. Was ah white sailor hat, three sizes too small. It couldn't even go over me forehead. When ah put it on, ah look like ah tube ah Colgate toothpaste. But de gloves was de best. We had some white gloves, 'bout ten size too small. When ah put dem on, dey could hardly go on, first dey tight. Ah had to bend all me fingers, an' keep dem bend like dat, if ah ever do so . . . gloves gone.

So see me Carnival Monday now, jumpin' up, tank-top stick inside me pants here, me body bend like ah Safety-pin to keep it dey, hat turn inside-out on top me head to make it fit me, an' me two hands curl up like claws to make sure de gloves stay on, an' ah jumpin' up like dat for de whole day. People only sayin', "Poor fella, ah wonder if he born so or he was in ah accident?" Ah say it must have more to carnival dan dat.

Den dey come an tell me how ah play wit' de wrong professional. Dey say, "Boy, what yu really have to do is go an' play with Edmond Hart!" Dey say dat is band, he does play for fun, yu go enjoy yuself, plenty woman, nakedness, "yu go enjoy yuself, nice band!" Ah go an' sign up wit' Edmond Hart. Dat year Edmond play someting call' "Tribute to Broadway." De only section I could get into was ah section call' Mary Poppins. Dey tell me how I am a Chimney Sweep.

If you see de costume. Ah red an' white stripe pants. When ah put it on ah look like ah wukkin' Royal Castle sellin' chicken. An' den button hole here, button over dey. When ah button-up, ah twist like dat, like ah piece ah wire. Den dey put ah tank-top on me, tie ah long scarf wrap 'round me neck, like dey want to choke me to death, put ah red hat on me head, gimme ah broomstick, two white gloves, charge me 'bout four hundred dollars, an' tell me I am ah Chimney Sweep in Mary Poppins.

Den ah have to walk by meself from Cascade to Belmont to meet de band. Yu ever walk by yuself, in yu costume, in de middle of de road, on ah Carnival Monday? Embarassin'! Taxi stoppin, "Wha' is dat he playin'? " Little children callin' yu, "Mama watch ah mas' passin'!" People wavin' at yu. "Boy wha' yu playin'? Wha' band yu from? Yu band loss?" All kinda ting. Embarassin'! Now I know why people does take car to go an' meet dey band. Everybody 'fraid to walk by deyself in dey costume. Ah say it must have more to Carnival dan dat.

De nex' year now, dey tell me forget band, save yu money, forget Tuesday Mas', concentrate on havin' ah good time, an' de best time to do dat is in J'Ouvert. An' de ting to do, is to go an' jump up wit' Invaders, after dat yu dont have to do nutten, jus' go home an' sleep, Invaders is de ting. Ah ask dem where Invaders comin' out from. Dey tell me go up Tragarete Road ah go see plenty people walkin' roun' lookin' like dey loss', dat is where Invaders is. So ah go up dey, an' ah see 'bout ten thousan' people lookin' loss', ah say right, dat is where Invaders is.

Yu ever jump up wit' Invaders on ah J'ouvert mornin'? Is ah art. Dem specialise in slowness. We leave 'bout four o'clock de mornin', ah reach Independence Square aroun' ten, meet de other bands goin' back, we now reach down dey. An' everybody who jumpin' wît Invaders is like dey know everybody else. If you hear dem. Dey jumpin' up an carryin' on big conversation. "How de wife? Children in school yet?", "Yu have visitors dis year?", "Ah forget de stove on, but ah eh goin' back at all, de house could burn down!", "You is Mr. Johnson daughter, ah eh see de family for a long time. How yu mudder? She dead? How yu father?

He dead too? How yu sister? She dead too? Ae, ae, all ah allyu dead, wha' happen, you dead too?"

An' while dis conversationisation takin' place, everybody tryin' to jump up near de band to get de sweet music. An' de panmen like dey feel dem people eh have deodorant, dey dont want dem near dem at all. Dey pushin' de pan thru' de crowd like is lawnmower dey have, an' people scatterin' left, right, an' centre, but dey still dey wit' de band. Ah nearly break me foot 'bout six time near Laperouse Cemetery, ah pan run over me heel, me foot go down in pothole, in manhole, if yu see me, jumpin' over drain, jumpin' over box', jumpin' over bottle. Ah spend de' whole J'Ouvert mornin' tryin' not to go in hospital. Half dem people yu see jumpin' high so, is not de music have dem so yu know, is dey bigtoe dey tryin' to save. But dey still wit' Invaders. Ah say it' mus' have more to Carnival dan dat.

De followin' year now, ah say ah not goin' to town at all, ah go stay home an' watch Carnival on TV. But friends as usual, find dat is ah waste of time. Dey say, "Well if yu go watch mas', why stay home? See it in livin' colour. Come down wit' us by de Savannah, is de best ting, we go sit down under ah Banyan tree, watch de mas, drink we rum, an' eat plenty food. What more yu want dan dat?" Ah say o.k. It wasn't ah bad idea, but de problem was de food. Dey bring Souse. Now Souse is ah funny ting, is not any an' everybody could make Souse. If yu see de Souse. Ah dont know where dey get de pig, but it was like ah pig of great experience, hard. An' de souse had so much hair on it yu could ah comb it, like dey never clean de pig. Ah say dese people tryin' to kill me.

Ah say it mus' have more to Carnival dan dat.

Well de followin' Carnival ah say ah takin' it light, ah eh goin' an' eat no bad food again. Den me partner in Rotary tell me, "Why yu dont come an' help we in de Bar? Is de best place to be. Yu could lime all day, talk-up nice woman, an' yu could see all dem Bands when dey passin'!"

Well boy, dat was ah mistake. Yu ever work in ah bar servin' Trinidadians? Never in dis life again. Dem people is someting else. Ah mean yu tryin' to do yu best, big band comin' down de road, 'bout five thousan', thirsty, natives want someting to wet dey throat, an' all ah dem want it at de same time, an' yu tink dey care? Care where. Ah man say, "Ah want ah beer!" Poor you push down yu hand in de barrel to get ah beer. Yu ever put yu hand down in ah barrel ah ice-water to get ah beer? Temperature down dey 'bout ten below zero. Yu hand near freezin' off. Ah bring up ah Carib. Cold. Hear him, "I dont drink Carib, ah want ah Stag!" Ah nearly knock him down. If he think dat I was puttin' my hand back dey for he, he lie. Hear me, "All Stag done is only Carib it have!" Who tell you he eh drink Carib! Not me an dem. Dey callin' yu all kinda, ting, "Aye you. Big head. Watch me over here. Yu deaf or what? Yu dont serve 'left side'? Ah want three paper cup wit' ice, no make dat five. An' two Rum an' Coke, an' ah Red sweet drink. Don't forget de straws. Yu have change for ah Hundred?" Me an' bar? Ah say it must have more to Carnival dan dat.

So ah take ah long rest from Carnival after dat. Den Minshall come on de scene, an' me troubles start again. Quite where ah livin', quiet at home, dey come by me. If you hear dem, "Forget dem oletime Bandleader, go an' play wit' Minshall, play Concept, progressive mas'. Ah go by Minshall. Well, when yu go by Minshall an' dem kinda big bands, yu dont look at de costume first, yu look at de prices. So ah bend down so, an' ah goin' down de line lookin' at prices — six hundred, five hundred, three hundred — when ah reach by my kinda price, about fifty dollars, ah look up to see wha' dat is. Ah say dat is my section, fifty dollars.

Dat year Minshall play Zodiac. My section was call' de Milky Way, was ah kinda Fancy Sailor section, all white, an' Minshall put all kinda stars, an' stars, scatter bout de pants foot, so me two foot look like ah fire-cracker dat gone off, all me foot star-up. An' on top ah dat, he design someting like ah Spiderman Mas!. Yu know de kind ah net-business Spider-man does wear in de Comic Books? He design dat. De ting look nice in de drawin', but try an' put it on. Is only ah man wit' ah straight nose could design someting like dat.

When I put on Minshall Spiderman Mas', me nose flatten down, me lip spread back, me ears wrap around, me eyelash gone inside me eye, all me hair come down over me forehead, an' people lookin' at me as if ah goin' an' rob de Bank, like in dem movies, we all goin' down de road like dat, like Bank Robbers. Well boy, we had to wrap it up, an' roll it up, an' put it on we head. An' people only lookin' at us an sayin', "Allyu wearin' stocking on allyu head!" Ah say it must have more to Carnival dan dat.

Dats when dey encourage me to become ah Stormer. De nex' year dey tell me, "Boy, listen, do like me, don't join no band, put yu money in yu pocket, put yu food dey, an' go an' stand up on Victoria Avenue, an' lime. An' every band dat pass, jump in it. So yu jump in an' yu jump out, dat way yu could jump up wit' every band in town for de whole Carnival, an' yu eh payin' no money."

Ah say dat is my kinda mas'. So ah gone on Victoria Avenue, an' ah limin' dey, waitin' for dem band to come down. But ah make ah mistake, ah jump in de wrong band first. Ah see dis big band comin' down de road, about ten thousan' people in de band, an' everybody in de band weighin' over three hundred pounds — McWilliams comin' down de road — an' he playin' some kinda fruits an' vege-tables, Breadfruit, Dasheen, Yam, Hibiscus, all kinda ting, real Agriculture comin' down de road.

But I didnt know dat. I jump in de Potato Section. Ah jump between two three-hundred pound potato. Dey mash me flat. De last ting ah remember, as dey puttin' me in de Ambulance on me way to hospital, was ah fella sayin', "Is like he play in de Mash Potato Section!"

TOP SOIL

Miss Maisie stared at her little garden in despair. It seemed that when God was sharing out soil he had completely for-gotten her. Everything she planted seemed to grow for a while, then just simply withered away. It was the soil, every-body told her it was the soil. No good they said, not enough 'vitamins' in it.

But Miss Maisie still tried. Every morning you could see her frail, bent figure, stooping among the beds where she grew the vegetables which she took to sell in the local market every Satruday morning, rain or shine. Her wrinkled face was always smiling, and she called out to villagers as they passed going about their various activities. They in turn called out to her, "How it goin' Miss Maisie? Yu still tryin' to grow stone? We dont want no hard vegetables, yu know!"

Miss Maisie just smiled and waved, and sometimes would answer in her high-pitched voice, "Never mind, de Lord go' take care of dis garden. One of dese days dis garden go' surprise allyu!"

It was Kevin, the little boy who lived next door that put the idea in Miss Maisie's head. Now Kevin was thirteen years old, a very bright thirteen. He was always listening to 'big people conversation', and always talking in a mysterious way, as if he knew all the top secrets in the world and didnt dare divulge them, but wanted you to know that he knew.

One morning he stopped by Miss Maisie's fence, and watched her for a few minutes as she dug and weeded among her vegetables. Then in his usual wise and conspiratorial way he said, "Yu know Miss Maisie, what yu really need in dat garden is some top soil. If I was you ah would get some top soil from up by Mr. Decarie, an' spread it all over dem beds yu have dey. Ah bet yu in no time at all yu garden win first prize in de Prime Minister Best Village Competition!" And with that, Kevin went his merry way, no doubt to advise some unsuspecting grown-up on some aspect of worldly affairs.

But he left behind a very thoughtful Miss Maisie. It had never occured to her to bring in new soil for her garden. She had tried putting things like cow dung and other kinds of manure, like everybody else, but nothing seemed to work. Her vegetables still came out looking as if they were suffering from a bad case of malnutrition.

One fella even told her one day, "Miss Maisie, if yu put more cow dung in dem beds, is cows yu go' grow, not vegetables."

The top soil idea suddenly appealed to Miss Maisie. But from Mr. Decarie? No way! Mr. Decarie had a small farm on the hill directly above Miss Maisie. And just as Miss Maisie's land didn't seem to be able to grow anything, Mr. Decarie's seemed as if it could grow just about everything. His whole farm looked green and healthy, the trees growing like they wanted to come right out of the ground.

But Mr. Decarie was something else. A short, red, portugese-looking man of about sixty years, he had a reputation of being mean and stingy, and got along with nobody. As a matter of fact, he was always threatening to shoot somebody for trespassing on his 'domicile'. Everybody said farm or property, or land, but Mr. Decarie referred to everything that he owned as his 'domicile'.

Miss Maisie gazed up the hill at the prosperous-looking farm for a while, then she made up her mind, she was going up the hill to ask Mr. Decarie for 'some top soil, please!' After all, the worse he could do was say no. But on second thought, he might also shoot her for trespassing.

She thought of tying a white cloth on a stick, like how she saw them doing in the movies when they wanted to show that they came in peace. But then she said to herself, "To hell wit' Decarie, man, ten like he can't shoot me!" And with that Miss Maisie put away her garden tools, went inside and changed her clothes, put on her best hat, and headed up the hill to see Mr. Decarie.

Mr. Decarie saw her coming up the hill, and got sour right away. Because he knew that it was something she wanted from him. Nobody ever came up there unless they wanted something. So in his mind he started saying 'no' already. He was sitting on the verandah when Miss Maisie rounded the corner of the house, a little out of breath after her climb up the hill.

He had a feeling to say 'no' and end the scene right there, but he prided himself on being of better stock than the rest of the villagers, and was therefore supposed to be able to handle every situation with diplomatic tact, always being sure that the end result was a big, fat 'no'!

Miss Maisie, on the other hand, suddenly began to have a change of heart. Before even a word was exchanged she began saying to herself, "But is why I come up here for? Ah should ah stay down de hill where I happy. Now dis man go' feel I come to beg he!" She took off her wide hat and began to fan with it. Then without really looking directly at him, she said, "Morning Mr. Decarie. But is like ah gettin' ole. Dat hill nearly kill me!"

Mr. Decarie grunted, took out his pipe, and said, "Morning Miss Maisie, what brings you up this way so early in the day?" Miss Maisie leaned up against the house, still fanning, and replied in a matter of fact voice, "Mr Decarie is no big ting. Jus' ah lil favour ah want to ask yu. Me garden down de hill catchin' it tail. People tell me is de soil, how it not good, an' how ah should get some top soil an' put it down in me garden to encourage de ole soil to stop playin' de fool, An' seein' as to how you is de only man roun' here wit' good soil, an' plenty soil to boot, ah was wonderin' if yu could let me have some. Not much, jus' 'bout ah half ah load!"

Mr. Decarie felt like hittin' de woman ah lash, but he didnt, he just sat there playing it cool, and organising the 'no' in his mind. He sucked on his pipe thoughtfully for a half a minute, then he said, "Miss Maisie there is nothing I would like more than to give you some top soil. As a matter of fact, if it was up to me, I would give you two truckloads, not just a half. But you see this land doesn't really belong to me, it belongs to the family. I just can't give away top soil just so, without the permission of all members of the family, and they are not here at the moment. ."

Mr. Decarie paused for a moment, seemingly to suck on his pipe, but really to see how Miss Maisie was taking the development of his 'no' so far. He wasn't quite sure, because she was still fanning with the hat, and wasn't looking at him directly, but seemed to be looking out into the distant mountains; though he was sure she was all ears to what he was saying.

He continued, "Yu know, Miss Maisie, top soil is not just top soil, it's land. And I cant give away family land, according to the terms of the Will, without full agreement of all owners of the land, which is the family. According to Article Seventeen of the Land Tenants Act, I could lose my government subsidy if I give away land without the proper authorisation. Is only God could give away land just so, because is God make land. I really sorry!" ··

Miss Maisie sat there listening to the rigmarole story that Mr. Decarie was telling her. She knew it was a lie, but her face didnt show it. She just smiled and nodded as he spoke, almost as if she knew that what he was saying was true, and was agreeing with him, and really should have known better than to come and ask for top soil.

She stayed for a few minutes making small talk, then she said, "Well Mr. Decarie, ah sorry ah bother yu head dis early mornin'. Is like ah go' have to look elsewhere for me top soil. But if yu ever get together wit' yu family, don't forget yu neighbour, yu hear? Mention me top soil for me. Ah gone!" And with that, she got up slowly, settled the hat firmly on her head, and started down the hill.

Mr. Decarie watched her as she made her way slowly down the hill. He smiled to himself, mentally congratulating himself on the handling of the situation. Suddenly he felt a drop of water splash on his high, arched nose. He looked up quickly as other drops followed. It had begun to rain. He suddenly realised that while he had been busy putting off Miss Maisie, it had become quite overcast. Quickly knocking his pipe out in the palm of his hand, he beat a hasty retreat inside the house, muttering to himself about 'the blasted rain' and how he "hope it pass soon."

The rain caught Miss Maisie halfway down the hill. She paused for a while, trying to make up her mind whether or not to seek shelter under one of the big Mango trees on the hill. But then she remembered that some of these showers had a habit of going on, and on, and on, as if they were playing games with people's lives.

She had no desire to spend 'no set of hours under no Mango tree', so she said half-loud to herself and the hill in general, 'Is home ah goin', man, ah could always dry-off. Me eh make out ah sugar, ah wouldn't melt'. And with that she pulled her hat a little more firmly down on her head, and shielding her face from the huge drops with her hand, she picked her way carefully down the now slippery track.

By the time Miss Maisie reached to her house she was soaked to the skin, and the rain was coming down like it really meant serious business. She dried off herself, changed to some clean, dry clothes, and made herself a nice strong, cup of Cocoa-tea. As she sipped it, she stood in front of her window watching the rain come down, and watching her nice little garden turn into a mud pond. Then she said to herself, "Dis eh no ordinary rain, it look like it go' fall till tomorrow!"

Miss Maisie was right, it rained steadily all day, with occasional wind, lightning, and peals of thunder which rattled the windowpanes. She turned on her radio around obituaries time, as she usually did every day, to find out if she knew anybody who may have passed away without her knowing. It was then she found out that the island was getting the effects of a tropical storm, which was passing a few miles off the coast.

When Miss Maisie turned in for the night it was still raining. She listened to the rain beating on her galvanise, and thought briefly of her poor little garden, Mr. Decarie, and the events of the day. There was not a thing she could do at the moment, so she just sighed deeply, said a silent prayer, put out the light, and drifted off to sleep.

It was about two in the morning, when Miss Maisie heard a terrific crash outside her house. She thought for a moment that the house had collapsed, but when she looked around her, everything seemed intact. 'Whatever it is go' have to wait till mornin' ' she thought, 'I not goin' out in dat dark for no jumbie to hold me.' She listened for a while. There was no more noise, and after a while she drifted back off to sleep.

The warm rays of the morning sun streaming though her window awakened her. She lay there for a minute, listening to the usual morning sounds that for the last sixty years, had been a natural part of her getting up to start another day. But there was something different this morning. She felt as if there was something she had to do but had forgotten, and couldn't remember what it was. She knew there was something she had to remember. But what was it? Was it a dream? Then like a flash it came to her. The noise in the night, that loud crash. She had to find out what it was.

She struggled out of her bed hurriedly, wriggled on her slippers, wrapped herself up in an old, worn housecoat, and headed for the front door. She slipped the latch, turned the key, and tried to push it open. It wouldnt budge. Something heavy was jammed against the door. Miss Maisie hurried over to her front window, to see if she could see what it was that was blocking her door. She pulled aside the curtain and peeped out. Miss Maisie's eyes almost popped our of her head in surprise. Her whole front yard, including her rocky little garden, was completely covered with the richest looking soil she had ever seen in her life. Right up to her front door.

It was soil from Mr. Decarie's estate. The heavy rains had loosened the soil, and the whole side of the hill had slid right down into Miss Maisie's yard. Miss Maisie stood looking for a moment, then she smiled as Mr. Decarie's words came back to her, "Is only God could give land just so, because is God make land!" She shook her head in wonder, made the sign of the cross very slowly, and very reverently, said "Thank you, God!" and went in to plan her day.

A PAN FOR CHRISTMAS (Theatre Script)

INTRODUCTION:

A Pan for Christmas is designed to be done in a variety of ways to suit the size of the group putting it on. Thus the music is interchangeable as the director wishes. For instance, instead of Parang, one can have Reggae or Cadence Christmas music. The three actors can play a variety of roles where there is a lack of actors. The Church scene can feature a soloist instead of a full choir. And the pre-show music presentation can be a separate feature or incorporated into the opening act. For instance, where a steel-band is available, the band itself becomes the pan-yard, and the actors work among the pans using the members of the band as part of the scene. Thus the show opens with a presentation of Christmas music by the band, after which the Narrator enters. It will be up to the director to start the action how he wants.

In this particular presentation, a full steel-band is set-up in front of the stage facing the audience. Platforms are set at the front of the band for the actors to play on in the first scene. Thus the band and actors are in the pan-yard, and Fargo is seen among them, directing them in their practice of Christmas Carols. During this, curtain on stage remains closed. After a few items, the full choir comes through the center of the closed curtain, and takes up its position alongside the band. Band and Choir do items together. Choir exits both sides, singing 'We Wish You A Merry Christmas'. Lights dim. Panmen remain among their pans. Narrator enters through center of closed curtain. Spotlight picks him up and he does the introduction. Lighting will have to be used to emphasise scenes of action taking place.

(AS LAST NOTES FADE AWAY THE STORYTELLER COMES ON AND ADDRESSES THE AUDIENCE. HE IS DRESSED AS AN OLD MAN.)

SCENE II

NARRATOR: It's so nice to see so many of you here tonight, reminds me of the Old Christmas days when we used to get together round a hot coalpot, an' cook an' tell Christmas stories. Well, tonight is going to be just like the ole days, and its a real nice night to tell a story. Tonight's story is called 'A Pan For Christmas', its all about a magic steelband pan. But you know behind every story there is another story, and so I am going to tell you the story behind the story. How many of you know how the steelpan was invented? Ah, there are many stories of how the pan was invented, but there is one that I like best. Want to hear it? Doesn't matter, I am going to tell it anyway. Sit back, relax, get yuself a drink but quietly, remember, a good story needs a good listener.

(PAN RAP – SLOW VERSION)

Once long ago
Not so long ago
An' de story ah tellin' is true,
Ah man take ah pan
Wit' ah hammer in he han'
Cool so he invent someting new.

Was ah ordinary drum
In which de oil used to come
It didn't make no particular soun',
One note maybe two
Yu could beat it till yu blue
Dat was all it could do for you.

Den dis man get dis plan
Wit' ah hammer in he han'

An' he say how he understan',
If de drum makin' one
An' de drum makin' two
Den de drum could well make
Quite a few.

So dis man take de pan
Wit' de hammer in he han'
An' he stoop down dey on de groun',
An' he heat it, an' he beat it
An' he stretch it, an' he mark it,
An' de pan start to make ah new soun'.

Music: Tune of Mary Had a Little Lamb; etc. one verse.
(Mimes Beating Pan)

Was ah do-re-mi, an' ah mi-re-do,
Dat was all he could make it play,
But it soun' so sweet
Dat he take it in de street
Was de fus time dey hear pan play.
An' all where he go, man, de crowd gather roun'
An' dey jump to de notes dat he poun'
An' none would forget
How dey dance an' dey fete
On de day dat de Steelband was born (Music: Mary etc.)

An' since dat time all over de lan'
Yu could hear de sweet soun' of pan,
For dey heat it, an' dey beat it,
An' dey stretch it, an' dey mark it
Like de man wit' de hammer in he han'

Dey make ah Tenor Pan
An' dey make ah Secon' Pan
Den dey come an' make a Double-Tenor, too,
Den dey make ah Alto Pan
An' dey make ah Cello Pan
Now it takin' sixty man to make ah ban',
It takin' sixty man to make ah ban.

104

Dey playin' do-re-mi
An' fa-so-la-ti-do
Ent no place de pan can't go,
Lower-Class, Upper-Class
Middle-Class, No-Class,
Classics to Kaiso.
Born on de streets of Trinidad
It has now gone far an' wide,
An' dey ent no stoppin'
An' dey ent no stayin'
It's de soun' of ah people's pride.

So when yu hear de beat
Of de Steelband in de street
An' de shuffle of ah tousan' feet,
Remember dat man
Wit' de hammer in he han'
Who put de fus notes on ah pan.
How he heat it, an' he beat it,
An' he stretch it, an' he mark it
As he stoop down dey on de groun'.
How he heat it, an' he beat it,
An' he stretch it, an' he mark it
An' de pan start to make ah new soun',
De pan start to make ah new soun'.

Music: Mary, etc. (Mimes beating Pan)

SCENE III PANYARD

(At the end of Pan Rap lights dim, spot
fades on storyteller, light comes up on
Fargo in Pan Yard set which has several
pans arranged as if for practice. Other
members of band in darkness. Tenor-Pan
on stand in spotlight. Fargo walks up to it.
Stands tense with pent up rage, looks as if
he wants to cuff the pan, but does not. He
raises his fists in frustration and shouts out.)

Fargo: Damn you! After all these years, all these blasted years, I still here, you still here, all ah we still here. After I do so much for you, what you do for me, eh? Ah have ah good mind to mash up yu arse. (Walks away from pan) Fifteen years I playin' pan. Dey eh have ah man in dis whole nation know pan like me. Fifteen blasted years, an' today dat woman have de gall to tell me I eh doin' nothin' with my life. (Thinks, Pauses) But she right, yu know, she blasted right. If ah had do like de rest ah dem, ah would ah have someting too. Someting real, someting like solid cash. But I is ah arse, I is ah real arse, ah love pan, oh how ah love pan. (Mimics) "Dis is ah alto pan sir, an' dis is ah tenor pan, sir. Dey does call dis de bass, sir, was invented in Trinidad. Could play anything sir, no sir, we not steelbandmen no more, we is panists, sir. De steelband has come ah long way." An' now de woman tellin' me ah eh do nothin' with me life? She right. She damn right.

(Soft Christmas music theme in, maybe steelband music, lights fade out on Fargo who is fiddling with pan. Lights come up on Narrator who is watching Fargo. Come All Ye Faithful by band in the background softly. Sometimes during play narrator takes audience's point of view.)

Narrator: Fargo was in ah bad mood. It was Christmas Eve, an' he hated Christmas Eve. Because dat was de one time ah year he used to feel like nobody eh like he. Because Fargo didn't have no family to like he. He mudder dead when he was six, an' he never even know who he father was. He grow up with ah ole aunt, he mudder sister, who everybody used to call Miss Silverina.

Fargo never used to like she at all, because she was always dey in ah church, mornin', noon, an' night, an' she used to drag Fargo along wit' she. So from de time he get big enough to make he own money, is because Fargo split-off from dat scene, an' rent ah lil bashee in Belmont. In no time at all, Fargo was one ah de baddest cats on de block. Everybody did 'fraid Fargo, an' dey never used to make no skylark wit' him. But dey did respect him, because Fargo had ah way wit' pan. As ah matter ah fact, dat was de only ting dat Fargo used to take any real interest in — beatin' pan. But what Fargo did like most 'bout beatin' pan, was de company in de pan yard. When he was in dey beatin' was like he had ah family, he used to feel like he belong somewhere. But Christmas was a different ting, because most ah de fellas had family, or outside chile, an' outside woman, an' Christmas was de one time dey used to ease up on de pan beatin', an' go an' spen' ah lil time wit' dey folks, an' bring present for de children. Fargo was de only one who didn't have no real place to go on Christmas Eve, except back to he bashee.

(Music out. Enter Splint. Lights go up on Fargo).

Splint: Wha' happenin' dey Fargo, boy? How yu lookin' so sour? Like is wha' ah hear is true?

Fargo: Wha' yu hear?

Splint: Ah hear is like you an' de woman on ah split.

Fargo: Is not de fus time, but dis time she really hurt me man, dat woman tell me some real hard tings. After all I do for she, boy dis world not fair.

Splint:	Well is like I tell you a long time ago, yu like pan more dan yuself. Get in on de action man, rise up an' wise up. Do like me, I wuks nowhere but I smokes duMaurier (Laughs).
Fargo:	Yu mean Marijuana.
Splint:	Ganja, herb, pot, marijuana, yu know ah better way to make ah few dollars?
Fargo:	An' ah better way to make ah jail? Yu see me an' dem police . . . All dey waitin' for is for me to make one slip, jus' one, an' is inside for me. Yu remember Panorama? Is only eyewitness dat save me from jail.
Splint:	But everybody know wasn't you dat start de fight, an' it wasn't even over pan.
Fargo:	Yu tink de police care 'bout dat? I name Fargo, ah have ah rep, anyting start an' I anywhere near dey, is me start it; yu bathe in de sea, fish bite yu, is shark. Dey jail me once, but not again, yu hear? Ah rather dead, an' me eh want to dead now, so I stayin' out dey way.
Splint:	Suit yuself, but remember, if yu want to make ah lil extra pesh de offer always open. (Enter Gloria)
Splint:	Ae, ae, Gloria girl, wha' happenin'? Long time no see.
Gloria:	I dey boy.
Splint:	If to say ah wasn't ah confirmed bachelor, ah woulda propose to yu right dis minute (Looks at Fargo) on second thought, ah might ah get me head bust, too. (checks watch on hand).
Fargo:	Wha' happenin' Splint, yu look like yu ready to go already, an' yu jus' reach.
Splint:	Ah can't stay too long, ah jus' want to run over de fus part of de tune.
Fargo:	Alright, alright, leh we try ah ting. (to Gloria) Yu playin'?
Gloria:	How yu mean if ah playin', an' ah come? (Vexish)

108

Splint:	But is wha' wrong wit' de two ah allyu? Is Tobago love or what? Why allyu eh kiss an' make up, ah go close me eye . . . . Yea man, allyu stop dis foolishness. (Pushes them together till they kiss)
Fargo:	Ok, ok lets get serious (Goes to Pans) allyu ready? (Light comes up on other members of the band) Take it from de top, an' remember allyu have to keep de rhythm. Ah one, ah two, ah three, ah four. (They play Rebecca or suitable calypso) No, no, not so! Allyu losin' de beat. Listen, la-la-la-etc: (Splint beats, Fargo listens) But wait nah, is like dat pan out ah tune, leh me see. (Examines Pan)
Splint:	(Looks at watch) Hear nah man, Fargo, ah have to split de scene. Yu know how dem ole folks stop. If ah eh drop in an' give dem ah hand on Christmas Eve, is ole talk for de res' ah de year.
Fargo:	Dats why allyu will never get anywhere wit' pan. Panorama jus' roun' de corner, an' you worryin' 'bout ole folks an' Christmas. Yu see me? Right now dis pan is de only ting dat important. Father Christmas can't help yu beat pan in Panorama, yu know. But if yu have to go, yu have to go.
Splint:	Boy, yu don't know my mudder, nah. Last Christmas ah promise to go Midnite Mass wit' she, an' ah forget, well is de whole year now I hearin' 'bout it. Every time I go dey, dat topic does come up. An' my wife worse. Dat woman is someting else. If ah eh help she put up dem drapes, me arse dark. Some ah she Parang friends comin' over to de house, an' is like she want to make de place look like de Arima Grandstan'.
Fargo:	Parang? An' we have pan to beat? As far as I concern, Parang is ah Spanish ting, an' it eh

have nutten to do wit' black people. Dem piole an' dem could keep it.

Gloria: Don't try dat! Allyu could talk allyu nonsense, but when yu touch Parang, yu touch me.

Splint: Wha' yu know 'bout Parang?

Gloria: Know 'bout Parang? Boy dat in my blood, boy, I born wit' dat. (Sings a verse and dances).

Splint: Well yea, nex' ting yu tellin' me yu name Glorietta not Gloria. (Laughs) But seriously Fargo, ah got to go now. We know de tune man, an' in any case, Christmas is only three days. As soon as Boxing Day done, is back in pan tail. Ah have to pick up ah lil someting for de chile. Is a big man now yu know, walkin' an' talkin', jus' now he go' start cussin! Wha' 'bout you Fargo, yu checkin' out de folks? Yu need some blessin' man, an' one way to get full blessin' is to help ole people at Christmas. After dat, suck eye, yu could get on bad all year, an' if yu dead, yu bound to go to heaven (Laughs).

Fargo: I alright man, don't dig nutten, ah go check allyu out later. (Splint starts to exit) Ah hope Santa bring someting nice for allyu (Laughter. Fargo goes up to Gloria and draws her close) Yu still vex wit' me?

Gloria: Man, Fargo you is someting else, yu does bring-off too much man.

Fargo: Ah sorry, but yu shouldn't say dem ting 'bout my panbeatin' man, dat is one ting I dont like nobody tell me nutten 'bout.

Gloria: Yu see you an' dat pan? Is someting else. But me eh sayin' nutten.

Fargo: Oh gorsh, forget dat nah, yu like to carry-on, eh? Yu see dat pan? One day dat same pan go make me man, you mark my words!

Gloria: Well maybe yu right, but yu got to straighten out yuself first, sometimes when yu tink is you

110

	beatin' pan, is pan beatin' you.
Fargo:	Well, is like de two of us spendin' Christmas together!
Gloria:	But Fargo, ent ah tell you ah have to go down San Fernando by me mudder an' dem? Ah does spen' every Christmas down dey. Ah does have to help Muds wit' de cake an' ting, yu know how it is? But yu could come too.
Fargo:	So is like everybody desert me. Sammy gone, Splint gone, an' now is like Christmas givin' me ah horn. In any case me eh get invite.
Gloria:	How yu mean get invite? You dont have to get invite by we, yu could come anytime yu want, yu know dat. As ah matter ah fact, dey tell me to make sure an' bring yu down, yu could spen' de whole Christmas by we, an' have Christmas Dinner an' everyting.
Fargo:	(Laughs) Me an' your family? No way. Fus ting ah know, ah go have to play gentleman an' talk proper, an' wear serviette, an' eat chicken wit' knife an' fork, an' say "grace before meals," an' "grace after meals", an' one set ah confusion. No sah, dat go spoil my whole Christmas, you could go if you want, I go stay here where I happy.
Gloria:	Is affair yu, but dont say ah never invite yu anywhere. (Kisses him, starts to exit) An' when yu go home check in yu bottom draw, it have someting dey for yu. I gone.
Fargo:	(Picks up sticks and plays a few notes, steups, and throws down sticks) To hell with all ah dem man, I know wha' I go' do. I go' go down town an' have ah ball all by myself. Who eh dead badly wounded. (Looks at the pan) Is like I desertin' yu too, boy, life strange, yes. (Exit)

SCENE IV DOWN TOWN

(Curtain on stage is now drawn open to reveal Down Town set. Sound effects/ some members of choir play vendors. Spotlight on Narrator).

Narrator:Was 'bout six o'clock in de evenin' when Fargo leave home. (Traffic) He decide he eh go' take no taxi, but dat he go walk (Sound effects) from Belmont to town an' just take he time, because he wasn't in no particular hurry. As he start to walk down de road, he could feel de Christmas spirit round him. Dey had people in de road like was carnival, an' everybody hurry hurry, like when yu stir up ah ants nest, an' dem ants get mad. An' everybody have parcel in dey hand, an' box on dey head, an' was like everybody talkin' at de same time, an' nobody listenin'. An Christmas music blastin' down de place from dem DJ record shop, an' dem car radio. An' dem taxi drivers self, doing dey level best, to see if dey could kill-off some more people before Christmas Day reach. Dey even had ah television van on de scene, an' ah lil girl wit' ah microphone askin' people wha' dey tink 'bout Christmas.
Fargo had to laugh when he hear some ah de answers (Enter girl with mike, interviews characters Actors or members of choir play characters).

1.
Interviewee   I definitely find dat Christmas is gettin' too commercial, everybody only studyin' wha' dey could get instead of rememberin' de true meanin' of Christmas, de birthday of de Lord. Is only buy, buy, buy an' fete, fete, fete. In de

ole days it never used to be so, we used to sing carols, an' go to church, an' bring gifts for de poor an' so on, but nowadays if yu poor, yu arse dark. (Pulls away mike) Is time to put Christ back into Christmas (Interviewer fights for mike).

2.
Interviewee   Christmas is de Birthday of de Lord an' I definitely find we should get ah extra day holiday for dat, yu see I likes to go to de beach for Christmas, but by de time me an' my husband drive up to Maracas, an' settle de children, an' begin to enjoy weself, time run out. So I find de extra day would be ah big help.

Interviewer   Excuse me, Miss, but where do you work?
2.   I works no where.

3. Rasta   Well, yu see, I an' I man dont really dig up on no Christmas. Is ah real dread scene, but I an' I have to get involve, because I-man have some hard goods to sell, is de hardest, so is dat kind ah scene I on. Never mind de place smellin' stink, an' it kinda nasty. Dat is not I-man fault, is Babylon dat dont send no garbage truck to pick up I-man stuff. Anyway love still, I-man forwardin'. (Shouts) Hail Jah Rastafari, Selassie I, ever livin', ever lovin', guidance!

4. Indian   Well lady, I is ah Indian, an' we Indians dont really celebrate Christmas. We more into Divali, an' Hosay, an' dem kind ah tings. But I is also ah Trinidadian, so if everybody feteing, I feteing too (Sings Marajiñ to Crowd).

Narrator: An' so dey carryin' on. An' while dey talkin', ah set ah limers only tryin' to get dey face in front de people camera. All over de place action takin' place. Even de carollers was out in full force. As ah matter ah fact, is dat wha' make Fargo stop at de corner of Queen an'

Charlotte Street. (Enter Parang-side) Dey had ah small side dey blastin' out one set ah Parang at de top ah dey voice, shakin' chac-chac like dey mad, an' carryin' on at ah rate. (Parang side does a series of songs. Narrator joins in fun).

Narrator: But what attract Fargo de most, was ah funny-lookin' little man wit' ah bushy-lookin' beard, who look like ah real Coco-Piole (Narrator goes up to little man and interviews him).

Narrator: Sir, are you a Coco-Piole?

Little man: I is ah Coco-Piole.

Narrator: You is ah Coco-Piole?

Little man: Hear nah man, leh me tell yu someting, yu see my great granmudder? She come from St. Joseph, yu know de ole Spanish capital. An' me granfadder on me fadder side come from Venezuela, yu understan?

Narrator: So wait nah, is how you come out so?

Little man: Well, hear nah man, yu see, is like me granfadder on me mudder side is ah Vincentian, an' I get de hair.

Narrator: Well, if you is ah Coco-Piole, den I is French an' Welsh.

Little man: (Shouts) So why yuh en go to France eh?

Narrator: Aye, wait nah, yu can't talk to me any ole how yu know, I is ah good mix, watch meh hair, yu see how it goodish, goodish?

(Members of group come over to get interviewed too. They all try to shout into mike).

1. I is ah Spanish Chinese.

2. An' I is quarter Indian.

3. An' I is Dougla.

4. An' I have Carib in me.

5. An' on top yuh too (Laughter).

6. An' my fadder come over on de same boat wit' Columbus.

7. De MV Tobagò. (Laughter).

Narrator:	He was de liveliest one ah de whole bunch. He was singin' away at de top ah he voice, an' jumpin' up an' down in time to de music. But what Fargo noticed de most, was de Tenor Pan de little man had round he neck. It was de most beautiful Tenor pan Fargo ever see in he life. It look as if it make out of silver an' gold. It didn't even have one lil dent in it. Everyting was smoothe, smoothe, just like baby bumsie. An' as de little man move about, de pan catch de sunlight an' reflect it in Fargo eye, as if de pan was woodfire wit' plenty sparks flyin' out de smoke. De inside ah de pan was jet black, so much so, you could ah hardly see de notes raise up on de pan.
	Fargo eh even stop to wonder wha' ah Tenor-pan doin' in de middle of ah Parang band. All he could ah study was de beauty ah de pan, an' de fact dat de little man was playin' some real off-key notes. Now if dey have one ting Fargo can't stand, is to hear somebody playin' bad pan. So without even tinkin' twice, Fargo walk up to de little man an' say . . .
	(Parang music continues softly, choir freezes action)
Fargo:	Here nah man, is like yu playin' dat wrong yu know, yu holdin' de stick an' dem wrong.
Little man:	Is what you know 'bout pan?
Fargo:	Man, I is pan fadder. Wha' me eh know 'bout pan eh worth knowin'. I cut me eyeteet on pan. De way yu holdin' dem stick, is like two chicken foot yu have in yu hand (Takes sticks) Yu have to hold dem not too tight an' not too light. Yu have to feel dem in yu han' like dey is alive, otherwise yu go choke de notes. (Plays) But dis pan is ah sweet pan, man, it have good tone, but is where yu get dis pan from?

115

Little man:	Ah make it meself, ah is ah boss at makin' ting. Yu should see me wukshop, yu should see how much ting ah have in it. Is so yu mean? (Hits the pan some bad notes).
Fargo:	Nah man yu still doin' it wrong, here let me show yu. (Takes pan) Right, now watch me (Runs scale) One ting ah could say for yu, is dat yu mightn' know how to beat pan, but yu sure know how to make dem, yu tink yu could make one so for me? As ah matter ah fact, ah few, ah have ah band yu know.
Little man:	Well, I don't really know, I is a busy man, an' I does only come dis way once ah year round dis time, besides is not only pan I does make yu know, I does make ah whole set ah ting. So much so, ah does have ah set ah lil fellas helpin' me all de time. (Choir unfreezes).
Narrator:	Fargo didn't want to ask too much questions, because he didn't want de little man to tink he farse. So he just stand up dey hittin' notes on de pan an' testin' it out, an' de more he play de pan is de more he like it. Dat was de best pan dat Fargo ever hold in he hand, in all de days dat he been beatin' pan. By dis time now sun set, an' darkness come down, an' de place begin to look like Christmas, with all dem Christmas lights shinin' all over de place an' in dem shop window. De little man stand up dey watchin' Fargo, not sayin' nothin' den he say:
Little man:	What ah nice young fella like you doin' all by yuself on ah night like Christmas Eve?
Fargo:	Me eh have no family man, I is de Lone Ranger, an' in any case me eh need nobody, I is Fargo.
Little man:	Dont need nobody? Ridiculous! Everybody needs somebody. Christmas is ah time of joy, of rememberin', of givin', of cheerin' others. You feel yu eh need nobody, but remember

	somebody may need you. If nobody could make you happy, den you make somebody happy. Yu sure yu dont have any family?
Fargo:	Only ah ole aunt, an' me eh see she for years.
Little man:	Why not drop in an' see she tonite? Is Christmas, an' she might love to see you. You cant never tell wit' Christmas, yu know, is ah time ah magic. Strange tings does happen, I could tell you story you would never believe. I is ah man travel far an' see ah lot.
Narrator:	As de little man speak, he eye take on ah far away look, an' suddenly, as if he embarass, he pull out ah big red handkerchief, an' he blow he nose loud, loud. Den is like he get ah new set ah energy, an' he begin to hustle an' bustle again, sayin':
Little man:	Ah got to go now, ah have to catch up wit' de others, we have lots to do tonight.
Narrator:	He put out he hand, an' almost reluctantly Fargo give him back de beautiful pan. De little man put it round he neck, den givin' Fargo ah right, he hurry down de road in de direction dat de Parang group had take. But, just as he reach de corner, he turn an' look back at Fargo. Den he wave an' shout out:
Little man:	Merry Christmas, an' remember to go an look for yu aunt!
Narrator:	An' dat was de last dat Fargo see of him, ah busy little figure, wit' ah Tenor-pan danglin' round he neck, disappearin' into de crowd. (Exit Little Man and Parang Group) Fargo stan' up dey for ah while, den he shake he head, shove he hand in he pocket, an' head for Independence Square. (Choir does Vendors song). All over de place Christmas Eve shoppin' was in full swing. Fargo walk slowly down Frederick Street, every now an den somebody would give him ah right or shout out to him.

Voice:	'Fargo, boy, wha' happenin'? Come an' fire one!
Narrator:	But Fargo wasn't in no mood to take no drink. What de little man had say to him was runnin' through he mind.
Voice:	"If nobody could make you happy, den you make somebody happy"
Narrator:	Fargo keep on walkin', an' next ting he know, he find heself outside de Cathedral on Independence Square. When he check de time, it was about eleven o'clock. (Chimes begin) He stand up dey outside de church watchin' de people goin' inside for Midnite Mass, an' guess what happen next? Dont worry I will tell yu, but I have to wet de throat ah lil bit, so dont go away, I'll be right back. (Exits as vendors song come to an end and curtain closes).

I N T E R M I S S I O N

SCENE V CATHEDRAL

Narrator:	Well as ah was tellin' yu all, Fargo find heself outside de Cathedral on Independence Square. Was 'bout eleven o'clock (Chimes). He stand up dey outside de church watchin' de people goin' inside for Midnite Mass. Same time de organ strike up, an' he hear de choir start up ah carol. (Curtain draws on church scene. Choir does series of Christmas Carols as the director sees fit. Organ or recorder music can be featured here). As Fargo stan' up dey listenin' to de music, he mind run on he aunt, an' he remembered de last ting de little man had say to him. "Merry Christmas, an' remember to go an look for yu aunt," an' sudden so, Fargo decide he goin' an' look for he aunt, an' he shout out, taxi!

SCENE VI TAXI

(Narrator puts on cap and number-plate round his neck, and becomes the Taxi-driver. He mimes driving round the stage, and comes to rest facing audience. Fargo in the meantime is walking up and down shouting 'taxi.' Taxi-driver mimes screech of brakes if sound effects are not available).

Taxi Driver: (Screech of brakes) O God yu want to dead or what? Yu eh know better dan to stan' up in de road to flag down taxi? Is like yu have insurance, where yu goin'?

Fargo: Diego Martin.

Taxi Driver: (To crowd) Christmas is ah time ah magic in truth, imagine he get ah Deigo Taxi easy so. (To Fargo) Diego Martin at dis time of night? OK jump in before ah change meh mind. (Drives off goin' round stage in circle with Fargo behind miming being inside a taxi) Yu feel how nice she runnin'? Ah just get ah tune-up, plus ah have in new shocks! (Screech of brakes, stops suddenly).

Fargo: Is like yu have in new brakes too, ah say Diego Martin yu know, not Belgrove Funeral Home.

Taxi Driver: Wha' happen, yu colour blind or what? Yu eh see de traffic light change colour? Dis is one time ah year me eh want to bounce nutten, an' me eh want nutten bounce me! Anyway, no big ting, ah know dis light, is ah true, true, stop light. When yu hear it say stop, it mean stop, for good. Till it ready to change. An' ah know it eh changin' in ah hurry. We have plenty time, so leh we fire one! (Pulls out rum flask, drinks and passes it to Fargo) (To audience) Christmas is ah time ah magic in truth, imagine ah taxi-driver givin' free drinks!

Fargo: (Drinks and makes ah face) But is what yu have in here boy, dis ting taste like embalmin' fluid.

119

	Yu sure yu not ah dead man drivin' round givin' free drinks?
Taxi Driver:	Dont be stupid boy, dat is wha' dey does call "Jack Iron" from down de islands! Dat could cure small pox, dengue fever an' cancer. I know, I drinkin' it for years, an' ah eh catch nothin' yet. (Drinks) Is de damn ting self. (Enter pedestrian with roll of linoleum).
Pedestrian:	Taxi, taxi, take one .... Diego!
Taxi Driver:	Ah full up.
Pedestrian:	How yu mean yu full up? Yu have plenty room, is only one maga fella yu have in dey.
Fargo:	Who yu callin' maga?
Taxi Driver:	Yu cant understan' English? Yu from France or wha'? Well ah go tell yu in Fringlish .... Ah fulla uppa ... Ah eh takin' no more passengers, ah done wuk for de nite.
Pedestrian:	Full up me arse, yu blasted fowl teaf, yu full ah shit. Ah blight mus' take yu. Yu feel yu could cut style on me, but dont try dat. If ah ever get ah place to put down dis linoleum, ah bus' yu arse. Allyu taxi drivers like to cut style an' show off on people when taxi scarce an' it late, but other times allyu does be beggin' we to drive in allyu motocar. But ah go' do for yu, ah know yu face, ah go ketch yu again. Let me see yu license plate. An' yu is ah blasted PH to boot! Is ok, cut yu style, monkey say cool breeze, come back, again. (Runs up and down, shouting, "Toxi, toxi!").
Taxi Driver:	But look meh crosses, my own taxi an' de man want to beat meh.
Fargo:	Is ah good ting he eh comin' here, ah dont know where he would ah put dat linoleum. But in any case is wha' he doin' wit' linoleum dis time ah nite?
Taxi Driver:	Yu could see yu young boy, yu have ah lot to learn. Christmas in not Christmas in Trinidad

an' Tobago unless yu have new linoneum on de floor. Yu eh bound to have floor, but yu bound to have linoleum. Remind me of one Christmas Eve, my mudder suddenly decide she have to paint de whole kitchen green. See me all over town Christmas Eve nite lookin' for green paint.

Fargo: Talk 'bout lookin', look wha' comin' now! (Enter lady laden with bags)

Taxi Driver: Is like dis lite stick, fus ah sorry ah eh break it now.

Lady: Sonny, yu goin' Diego Martin?

Taxi Driver: Well, ah not really, really goin' Diego Martin, ah only goin' part way. Ah kinda off-duty now.

Lady: Is ok, God go bless yu. Ah takin' de drop any where yu goin', meh foot is like it want to drop off.

Taxi Driver: But, is like yu buy de whole ah town. What yu doin' wit' all dem parcels? Next ting police charge me for drivin' without ah truck license.

Lady: Yu see dese parcels? If ah eh get dem home, well, is no Christmas for none ah we. One have de ham, de nex one have de scotch. Dis one have de last batch ah sorrel dey had in de market, an' dis one have dem children gifts. So yu see my whole Christmas inside dem bags here.

Fargo: Ok lady, come in if yu comin' in, come in, O' God!

Lady: Hold dis for me, (Loads Fargo with some bags etc. and settles in). (Enter pedestrian).

Pedestrian: Ah ketch yu! So yu eh have room? Well if yu takin' she, yu takin' me too, or not ah man goin' home tonite (Lays his linoleum down in front taxi).

Taxi Driver: Lord why me? Is like yu want to embarass de government? Dey cant find pitch to fix de road but you could find linoleum? Ok come in, come in, but mind yu jook out people eye wit' dat linoleum (Pedestrian gets into taxi with linoleum . Plenty commotion arranging the linoleum over everybody's shoulder).

Taxi Driver: I dont care whether dis lite change or not, I gone! (Drives off stage with everybody miming being in a taxi. Drives back on a few minutes later with only Fargo).

Taxi Driver: Tank God ah get rid of dem two. Between dem bags an' dat linoleum, dis car smellin' like Frederick Street after rain fall. How far yu goin'?

Fargo: (Suddenly) Drop me rite here!

Taxi Driver: (Screech of brakes) O God, yu want to kill me? Well yu reach! (Fargo leaves without paying)

Taxi Driver: Aye, aye like you forgettin' someting. Where me money?

Fargo: (Off Stage) Dat is my Christmas!

Taxi Driver: (To audience) Yu see why Christmas is ah time of magic? Cool, cool so, me money disappear. (Takes off cap and number plate and becomes Narrator).

SCENE VII AUNT'S HOUSE

Fargo is seen outside door. Aunt and neighbours are fixing up Christmas Tree. Aunt in rocker. Christmas music playing softly.

Narrator: When Fargo finally reach where he aunt livin', he stan' up outside de gate watchin' de house, an' he say to heself, "Boy ah really treat me aunt bad in trut' yes! Is ah good ting ah decide to come an' look she up." Ah lite was on inside, an' he could hear de radio playin', an' people talkin'.

(Inside House)

Neighbour 1 But Nen, how de Christmas treatin' you? Yu finish de bakin' yet?

Aunt:	All bakin' done, is de sorrel to draw now. Ah just put ah fresh batch to draw.
Neighbour 2	My sorrel done set, is de punch-o-creme ah have to worry 'bout now, ah tink ah lil bit short on milk.
Aunt:	I would ah finish ah long time child, but is de arthritis an' de fluid in me knee dat slow me down, long time all now so everyting finish. Ah was strong, plus ah had de three children.
Neighbour 1	But where de children dis year, nobody comin' home for Christmas?
Aunt:	De children too far dis year child. Michael in Toronto wid he new wife. He write to say how dis go' be he first white Christmas, although dey eh see no snow yet. Betty self in New York, she come last year, an' de year before dat, so she say she skippin' dis year.
Neighbour 2	An' wha' 'bout Fargo?
Aunt:	Fargo? Child ah dont know when last ah lay eyes on Fargo. From de time he leave dis house ah eh see him again. Ah read 'bout him an' de police once, but he was innocent, he get off. But he never come back here. Ah used to be strict with him, but was for he own good. He was a strange boy, always moody, but he mean well, I know dat. De Lord alone know where he is tonite. Ah have someting here for him.
Neighbour 1	At least you have ah excuse, your children away, but mine livin' right here an' ah dont even see dem. Every once in ah while, dey would drop by, but before dey turn round twice, dey watchin' dey watch like dey have appointment.
Neighbour 2	De tree lookin' real nice, but ah still say yu can't beat ah local tree. Remember when we used to use Whistlin' Willow? An' tree branch? An' we used to make we own decorations? Dese tings alright, dey pretty, but yu dont get

123

	de same joy as when yu make it yuself.
	(They stand back admiring the tree).
Aunt:	Hush! Is like ah hear somebody outside!
Narrator:	Fargo stan' up outside de house listenin' for ah while, den takin' ah deep breath he march up to de door an' knock. (Knocks) He hear de voices quiet down an' he aunt voice sayin'.
Aunt:	Who is dat?
Fargo:	Fargo!
Narrator:	Dere was silence for ah moment. Den de door open an' he aunt stan' up dey lookin' at him, she two eye open big, big, as if she see ah ghost. Den she say "Fargo," an' she burst out into one set ah tears. Fargo now start to lie.
Fargo:	Wha' happenin' aunty? Ah was in de area so ah decide to drop in an' say hello.
Narrator:	Well is now self he aunt start to bawl. Fargo self start to feel kind ah stupid, because he dont like to see people cry, plus she was wettin' up he good shirt. Den he aunt dry she eye an' say. .
Aunt:	Well wha' yu standin' up dey for, yu 'fraid de house? Come inside boy, (She pulls him inside) Is ah strange ting, mus' be de Lord send yu. Is only tonite me mind run on yu. Ah present come here for yu, an' ah was wonderin' how ah would ever get it to yu.
Fargo:	Ah present for me?
Aunt:	Yes, look it dey, ah lil man bring it.
Narrator:	Fargo look at de tree dat he aunt been pointin' at, an' he nearly drop dead. For lyin' right in de middle of all de presents was de beautiful Tenor pan, de same one dat he had help de man wit' down town earlier in de evenin'. Fargo hand begin to tremble so much, dat he could ah scarcely pick up de pan. An when he finally pick it up, he notice ah little note on de side in one set ah scrawlin' hand writin', like

124

when cockroach fall in ink an' walk over somebody Exercise Book. An' de note say, "Merry Christmas Fargo — if nobody could make you happy — den you make somebody happy" But dere was no signature. Fargo head start to spin with all kind ah thoughts.

Fargo: But how dis man know where I livin'? Me never tell he nothin'. Ah wonder who is dis lil man, boy? Huh, take care dis pan have obeah in it nah!

Aunt: Wha' happen to you? Yu never get ah present yet? Mus' be some woman who sweet on you. Never mind dat, play it leh me hear yu, nah!

Neighbours Play it!

Narrator: Den Fargo start to play de pan, an' as he play he begin to feel happier dan he ever feel in ah long time. An' all de neighbours come over to see wha' goin' on (Enter Choir) An' as de music full de room, he feel as if ah whole steelband was playin' (Steelband music), an' he say, "Merry Christmas, Aunty," an' he keep on playin' as de clock strike midnite. (Choir and everybody sing carol. Chimes)

(Narrator speaks over choir singing).

Narrator: Well, ah hope allyu like dis Christmas story, an dont forget "If nobody could make you happy, den you make somebody happy dis Christmas" — Merry Christmas! (Choir Cresceno).

HIGHWAY CODE

I tink is high time we take ah serious look at de drivin' situation in Trinidad & Tobago. Because de way people drivin' over here dese days, is like everybody have dey own Highway Code. I tink is important dat we examine de situation, an' try to come up wit' ah Highway Code dat everybody could live an' die by quite happily.

Let us first examine dis ting dey call de motocar. In de first place, when yu drivin' it, is a 'motocar.' When you bounce somebody, is ah 'vehicle.' Dats why yu does hear de police sayin' how, "de vehicle was travellin' from North to South, an' it came into contact wit' de victim." So you see, confusion already.

Yes sir, Trinidadians have ah strange relationship with dis ting call' de motocar. In de first place, dey eh fraid it at all. Dey does run from dog, dey does run from rain, dey does run from bullet, but dey don't run from motocar. Dey does stand up for motocar like dem is motocar Godfather. If yu hear dem, "Bounce me, nah! Bounce me, nah! Ah hope yu have insurance." Well dey cant say dat too often again, because de way insurance companies closin' down dese days, nobody sure if dey insure. As ah matter of fact, when you take out ah insurance dese days, yu have to take out ah nex' insurance to insure yu insurance.

Part of de problem between de people an' de motocar, is de fact dat it have too much motocar in de country. Just now it go have more motocar dan people. Imagine I go to ah fete de other day, it have 1000 people in de fete, an' 2000 motocar outside. Everybody come in two car. So yu see, people who walkin' feel insecure, dey feel threatened by de motocar. So dey always challengin' motocar. Some ah dem feel dat somewhere in de Constitution it say 'de road make to walk,' so dey does walk all over it, regardless of you an' yu motocar. I comin' down de road de other day, dese two, big fat women cross in front my car, den stop to talk, just so, in de middle of de road. So I beep me horn. Well, is who tell me do dat! One woman watch me one 'bad eye,' den hit me, "Yu cant wait? How yu hurry so, you dont have no manners? Yu cant see two big people talking? Yu goin' to wait yu hear? Yu is ah Russian or what?" An' she forget 'bout me. Yu tink it easy? An' dat not all, West Indians love to walk between motocars in traffic. Dey believe all cars have good brakes. Dats why so many West Indians have flat knees, wit' dey kneecap all behind dey heel. Dat's from walkin' between motocar in traffic an' gettin' squeeze

An' de dogs an' de pigeons jus' like de people, dey not movin' for nobody. Imagine over here motocar does bounce pigeon!

Yu see, ah lot ah people long for de good ole days, when all we had in town was donkeycart an' bycycle. Yu used to be able to take half hour to cross de road, because all yu had to worry 'bout was ah speedin' donkey-cart. But now it have motocar goin' one hundred mile per hour. Before yu do so, is gone yu gone. Yu know how much people reach de hospital, an' de last ting dey ever say is, "Ah thought ah could ah make it!"

An' de roads dont help neither. We have three kind ah road in de West Indies. Highways, By-ways, an' No-ways. . . dats for people who dont know where dey goin', an' dont care.

An' most of dese roads dont have flyovers or walkovers. Yu build walkover for dem here, an' dey crossin' de road over dey! Dey rather take dey chance wit' traffic. . Next ting car hit dem, an' dey turn 'flyover' immediately. So dont be surprise if every now an' den yu see somebody go flyin' over yu car. Is not Superman. Dat is ah native who dont believe in using walkover.

Now ah motocar can be very dangerous if yu dont know how to drive it. If yu dont believe me, check out de cemetery. Yu see tings like, "Here lies Dear John. Departed this earth on the 9th of November, in a Mazda" Yu must have some kind of intelligence, an' ah sense of judgement, to be ah good driver. But de way tings goin' dese days, is only stupid people gettin' to drive motocar.

Dis girl I know went for she drivin' test. Comin' down de

road, de Instructor tell her signal right . . she do so. Signal left . . she do so . . an' jook him in he eye. She fail. But she say how dey discriminate against her. She try again a second time. Dis time she fail de written part. Yu know dese days how West Indian governments love to build Roundabouts. Dey does do three tings when dey get into power — give a holiday, throw ah party, an' build ah Roundabout. Dey say is ah sign of progress. So we have plenty Roundabout Governments. Every island yu go to is ah set of Roundabouts. De other day ah fella was drivin' an' he spare tyre fall out. Yu know by de time he go back for it, he see people drivin' round it? Dey thought was ah new Roundabout now open.

Well sometimes dey does call dese Roundabouts 'Road Islands,' an' plant dem up with all kinda lawngrass, an' flowers, an' rocks, an' cactus, an' dey does put a sign sayin', 'maintained by so and do.' Well dey ask de girl "What is a Road Island?" she say, "A big red fowl!" Yu ever hear 'bout Rhode Island chicken? Dey fail she again. But she eventually get she license, because dey say it have people who more stupid dan she drivin', an' in any case, none ah dem want to take she up again, because dey fraid dey dead.

An' yu know two weeks later she nearly kill me. I passin' outside de girl house, sudden, sudden so, she back out in de road, without no kind ah signal, an' nearly mash up my good, good, motocar. So I say, "Girl is what wrong with you? You eh give no signal?" She say "Signal? Wha' signal yu talkin' 'bout? Everybody know I does back out here every morning."

So yu see, yu have to look out for all kinds of mad people. De Traffic Department say yu must learn Defensive Driving. But in Trinidad we believe dat de best defense is ah good offense, so we does try to bounce you before you bounce us. Dat's why is so necessary to understand de Trinidadian approach to de motocar. When we understand dat, it go' be easy to develop ah Highway Code more in keepin' wit' our needs. Which is what I workin' on right now.

For instance, when de Americans, an' de English people, an' de Japanese an' dem, send dey cars down here, dey does call dem tings like Hillman, Bentz, Ford, Mazda, Toyota an' all kind ah names. But by de time dey land in Trinidad all dat change. Basically we only have three kinds ah cars in Trinidad . . VOOM! VOOSH! an' BADAM! So you could decide which one it is you drivin.'

An' of course yu know, most West Indians dont know de size of dey cars. Yu does see some fellas wit' some long, long car tryin' to park in some small, small, space, dat even ah blind man could see too small for dey car. I see ah woman de other day, in ah Mini Minor. She tryin' to park. De woman have two acre of parking lot, one car park dey, she bounce de man car. Tell him how he park bad.

An' when you hear your car get hit, is horrors, because de cost of car parts dese days is someting else; man does bawl when dey hear de costs. As ah matter of fact, dey dont sell 'parts' no more, dey does sell someting call' 'kits'. If yu want ah door-handle, yu have to buy ah bumper an' ah back seat, dat's ah 'door-handle kit.' If yu want ah set ah points, yu have to buy ah chassis an' ah steering wheel, dats ah 'points kit.' Ah mean dey dont sell nothin' by itself no more, to get ah small washer so, yu have to buy half de car.

So much so, people gettin' kill' because car parts so expensive. Imagine, I buy ah pair ah Brake-pads de other day for one hundred dollars. One hundred dollars! So yu tink I mashin' brakes? Yu mad or what! If yu come in front me yu gettin' bounce. I not wastin' down my expensive Brake-pads to save you. Is joke yu makin'!

But one ting ah could say for Trinidad, is dat we is de land of Mechanics. No matter what kind ah car yu drivin', no matter where yu break down, mechanic does jump out of de bush at yu, "I could fix dat! I could fix dat! No problem, is de Carburetor!" Ah dont know where dey come from, spanner in dey back pocket, screwdriver in dey hand, I could fix dat, "Is de Carburetor!" Dats ah nex' ting. Yu ever notice is always de Carburetor? Even if is only ah puncture yu get, dey tellin' yu 'de Carburetor bad!'.

An' de Japanese people expensive motocar dat it take all kind ah computer to make, Trinidadians fixin' dem wit' nail, rubber band, hairpin, scotch tape, Evostick. But of course to be ah good mechanic in Trinidad, yu have to study music; dats why I know de Steelband will go on forever. Fellas go' always get work as mechanic, because if you dont know music yu cant deal wit' some ah we drivers.

Dey does come an' tell yu how, "De car goin' plinky, plinky, plinky!" An' how dey hearin' someting goin', "Ah-joogoo, ah-joogoo, ah-joogoo, underneath de steerin' wheel by de bumper dey so!" An' how, "Every time ah do so, de car do so!"

De poor mechanic have to figure it out by music now. Hear him, "If is plinky, plinky, is yu Carburetor. If is ah-joogoo, ah-joogoo, yu brake pads gone. An' if is blah-blah-blah, dat is yu wife in de back seat.

So yu see, we have ah special relationship wit' dis ting call' motocar, dats why we have to develop a Highway Code dat take dis relationship into consideration.

In de first place, when it come to drivin' on de lef' or drivin' on de right, dat dont apply to us at all, at all. We have someting call' 'All About Drive.' Dat mean if yu feel like drivin' on de lef ' drive on de lef ' if yu feel like drivin' on de right, drive on de right. If yu feel like drivin' in de middle of de road, dat alright too. As ah matter of fact, most people feel dat de middle of de road is de safest place to drive, an' dey does drive dey. Some of dem have what dey does call de 'Train-line mentality.' Dey long for de good ole days when we used to have trains; so anytime dey see ah white-line, dey say, 'O' god, train, ' an' dey jump on it, an' is gone dey gone, mashin' up people expensive motocar.

Now dis ting call' 'shoulder of road' dont exist at all. Over here 'shoulder' make to cry on, an' for taxi-drivers to pass. If you ever lose control of your car on de Highway in Trinidad, forget 'bout shoulder. Jus' head for de nearest Watermelon Stand! Trinidad is de only place I know yu could drown on de Highway, or dead as ah Fruit Salad.

On de question of parking, everybody know dat it basically have three kinds of parking in Trinidad. Pull-up, Stop, an' Abandon. Durin' de last clean-up campaign, plenty people report dey car missin'. But wasn't teaf dey get teaf, was decent citizens who pick dem up an' throw dem in de Labasse, because de way dey park, everybody thought dey didnt have no owner. It had ah time when man used to park dey car careful, careful, like ah baby, under light, well up on de sidewalk, so dat dey cant get hit an' tings like dat. But since dey get money, dey just jumpin' out car, an tellin' car, 'see yu later, take care of yuself.'

De nex' ting 'bout parkin' de code would have to consider, is parkin' by home. Well, you self know how Trinidadians does live all 'bout de place. So de old ting 'bout "no parking on de brow of ah hill" go' definitely have to go. De code go' have to state dat, 'If yu live dey, yu could park dey!' If yu live on top ah hill, yu could park on top de hill, if yu live round ah corner, yu could park round de corner. If yu are ah vagrant an' yu own ah car, an' yu live on de sidewalk, yu could park on de sidewalk. If yu live dey, yu could park dey!

Now if yu in Trinidad, an' yu see 'bout twenty cars park up on de Highway, do not panic. It could be three tings. Ah picnic on de way to Mayaro, ah N.A.R. motorcade dat loss, or ah Indian Wedding wit' ah puncture.

Approach all buses dat have singin', drummin', dancin', hymns, an tings like dat comin' out de windows, wit' caution. Yu might get hit wit' ah Bible, ah Rum bottle, or ah Roti.

If you see two drivers park up in de middle of de road, blockin' traffic, an' carryin' on conversation like dey havin' ah Summit Conference, do not panic. Be patient. Dat is democracy at work. In Trinidad we dont take no sides, we always stay in de middle. Dat is Foreign policy, an' dat is Domestic Policy too. We does take 'bout thirty years to change anyting, but we does change. So drivers dont pull to de side. De best ting to do is to go over an' join de discussion.

On de question of 'approaching vehicles' an' de way we drive, de Code go' have to read as follows. "If you are going down de road, an' ah man is comin' up, an' de obstruction is on your side, do not stop. Speed up. Who reach first, pass first." Over here we dont have no 'Right-of-way,' we only have 'right away,' an' after dat, 'Write-off.'

Now when it comes to de question of "overtaking," de Code will have to vary ah bit. It go' have to read, 'Who vex most, overtake first.' Dat mean if you more vex dan de nex' man, you could go ahead. But never overtake one car at ah time, not in Trinidad, dat is bad driving. Always try to overtake at least twenty cars one time, an' if you could squeeze in ah Concrete Mixer, dat would even make it better. An' always try to overtake round ah corner, because it has been proven dat dat is where dey always have de most room.

Now if you are drivin' up de Highway, an' you see ah car approachin' you on your side of de road, at about ah hundred miles per hour, an' de car flashin' it light at you, dat mean one ting. It mean dat man comin' thru' whether he have right-of-way or not. So you have to decide whether or not you givin' up your right-of-way. But dat make drivin' very excitin' in Trinidad & Tobago.

As far as hand signals are concerned, well all have to go. Because traffic goin' so fast dese days, dat if yu ever put out yu hand, it reachin' where you goin' before you. If yu see ah man do so, he goin' Belmont, if he do so, he goin' Diego Martin, if he do so, he goin' San Fernando, if he do so, he goin' Mad-House.

Now if yu drivin' behind ah taxi, an' yu want to know where de Taxi goin', never look at de Taxi-driver. Look at de frightened passengers in de backseat. Dey go' always be lookin', longingly, where dey supposed to be goin', an' if yu look dere, yu go know where de Taxi goin'. But if yu drivin' behind ah Rasta, yu could expect anyting, especially when it come to U-turns. Because Rastas dont obey 'No U-turns', dey only obey 'No I-turns'.

When it come to signs and so on, yu have to remember dat Trinidad is ah place where dey dont like to put up signs, jus' like de other West Indian islands. We like to use symbols like 'big tree,' 'round de corner,' 'by so an' so,' an' tings like dat. After all, we livin' here, so we know where we goin', an' where everybody livin'. Yu ever notice where people does put dere house number? Under de step, or de roof, or de verandah, where nobody could see it. So if you see ah sign sayin' "Detour," dont bother wit' it, dat is for de Tourists. You just go right ahead.

Now remember to watch out for Donkeycarts and bycycles, 'One Way' streets dont apply to dem. Dey does go up an' down as dey well please, because in de West Indies ah Donkeycart an' ah bycycle is considered an advanced form of pedestrian.

Now if yu drivin' behind ah bus, or a truck, or ah car wit' lumber stickin' out in de back, or ole iron stickin' out in de front, or bedpost, an' bedframe, an' ting stickin' out in de back, an' yu see ah red panty, ah red bra, ah red dress, ah red underpants, tie on to de end, remember dat is not Trinidadians dryin' laundry. Dat is ah danger signal. It mean dont come too close, or yu go get yu eye jook out. In most countries dey hang up flags, but we are ah wealthy country, so we hang out clothes.

Now if yu drivin' up de Highway, an' yu see ah big hole wit' plenty lights 'round it, remember is not Christmas or Divali. Dat is ah danger sign. It mean 'Danger, big hole, yu go dead.' Now if yu see ah big hole wit' no lights round it, it mean de same ting, but dont worry, yu go find out very quick.

When it come to lining up, especially in Traffic, yu must remember dat in Trinidad an' most of de other islands, we have someting called de 'fat line.' In most countries people usually line up one behind de other, we like to line up alongside each other. De only ting dat does line up one behind de other in de West Indies, is Ants. Dat come from slavery. Yu see, when dey catch us an' had us goin' up on de boat, dey had us goin' up one behind de other. Since dat time, we dont do dat no more. So dont get too frustrated when cars suddenly come alongside you or cut across yu in traffic, is really line-up dey linin' up.

Remember, if yu miss your turn-off, yu could always back-back on de Highway. Jus' blink yu lights, an' blow yu horn, an' speed up in reverse. When Sparrow say 'dont back-

back,' he wasnt refering to de Highway. If yu miss your turn, is not your fault really, everybody know is de Government fault.

Now if yu ever see ah Police Patrol, slow down an' look very carefully. Yu might never see another one in de rest of yu life. Finally, if yu drivin', an' yu drivin' fast, always try to drive at least one inch behind de car in front of you, especially if yu doin' 'bout ah hundred miles per hour. It goin' to prove dat you are ah very friendly person, an' dat yu would like to change yu address to de General Hospital.

Having said all this, an' now that you understand why we need dis new Highway Code, the important thing to remember is dis — If yu drinkin' dont drive, an' if yu drivin' dont drink, but dey have some people in dis country who would drive yu to drink.

GLOSSARY

Ah . . . . A, I, of.

All yu, allyu, all ah yu . . . . All of you.

Arima . . . . Borough of Arima, North East, Trinidad.

Bacchanal . . . . Confusion, scandal.

Bad-John . . . . Bully, violent person, criminal type.

Balisier . . . . Red and yellow colored flower.

Bashee . . . . Bachelor apartment, cramped quarters.

Basket . . . . To take basket, to be fooled.

BeeWee . . . . B.W.I.A. National Airline of Trinidad & Tobago.

Boxing Day . . . . The day after Christmas.

Carib . . . . Trinidad beer product.

Calaloo . . . . Popular dish similar to Spinach.

Chaguaramas . . . Western Peninsula, Trinidad.

Ciboney . . . . One of the original inhabitants of Trinidad & Tobago.

Coco-Piole . . . . Reference to Venezuelans, spanish-speaking people.

Cocoa-Tea . . . . Hot drink made with Cocoa.

C.O.L.A. . . . . Cost of Living Allowance.

Compound . . . . To polish car.

Confuffle . . . . To confuse.

Corbeau . . . . Cobo, vulture.

Craupaud . . . . Crappo, frog.

Dan . . . . Than.

De . . . . The.

Dem . . . . Them.

Den . . . . Then.

Dese . . . . These.

Dey . . . . They.

Divali . . . . East Indian Festival of Lights.

Dose . . . . Those.

Doubles . . . . East Indian delicacy.

Draw Sorrel . . . . To make the popular red Christmas drink.

Eh, ehn . . . . Am not/is not/are not.

Fa . . . . For.

Farse . . . . To pry, out of place, to take an unasked interest in someone else's affairs.

Fuh . . . . For.

Fus . . . . First.

Galvanise . . . . Zinc sheets used for roofing houses.

Go' go . . . . I am going to go.

Gypsy . . . . Calypsonian Winston Peters.

Hart . . . . Edmund Hart, Carnival Bandleader.

Hops-Bread . . . . Small round loaves, bread rolls.

Horn . . . . To be unfaithful to.

Hosay . . . . East Indian festival.

Indentured Servants . . . . East Indians brought to Trinidad & Tobago to work.

Invaders . . . . Popular Steelband situated in Woodbrook, Trinidad.

Is Affair You . . . . That's your business, suit yourself.

Jack Iron . . . . Strong White Rum found in the smaller islands.

Jep .... Wasp.

Jook .... To stick someone, to prick, prod.

Jorts .... Foodstuff.

J'Ouvert .... Carnival Monday morning, Jour Ouvert.

Jumbie .... Ghost, spirit.

Kinda .... Kind of.

Kind ah .... Kind of.

Leh .... Let.

Lemme .... Let me.

Maga .... Scrawny lookin, undernourished.

Maracas .... North Coast, Trinidad Beach.

Marse .... Confusion like carnival, to do in a grand manner, from Mask.

Mayaro .... East Coast, Trinidad Beach.

Me arse dark .... to be in trouble, no hope.

Meiling .... Meiling Esau, Fashion Designer.

Minshall .... Peter Minshall, Carnival Bandleader.

McWilliams .... Irvin McWilliams, Carnival Bandleader.

N.A.R. .... Political party, National Alliance for Reconstruction.

N.C.C. .... National Carnival Committee.

Neal & Massy .... Neal & Massy Ltd, business establishment in Trinidad & Tobago.

Nutten .... Nothing.

Nyam .... To eat greedily.

Obeah .... Black magic, witchcraft.

Old Oak .... Brand of Trinidad Rum.

Panorama .... Steelband competition held at Carnival.

Parang .... Spanish type music played in Trinidad during the Christmas season.

PauPau .... Papaya, fruit.

Pelau .... Dish made from rice, peas and meat mixed together.

Pesh .... Money.

PH Taxi .... Private car used for hire.

Pitch marble .... To play the game of marbles.

Pommerack .... Red pear-like fruit.

Punch-O-Creme .... Christmas drink made from milk, rum, eggs and other ingredients.

Rasta .... Reference to the Rastafarian group of Jamaica.

Rigmarole .... Confusion, disorganisation.

Rotary .... Rotary Club, businessmen's service organisation.

Roti .... East Indian dish, popular meal.

Saldenah .... Harold Saldenah, Carnival Bandleader.

Savannah .... Large park and playing field in Port-of-Spain.

Scrunt .... To be down and out, seeing hard times.

Sorrel .... Popular red Christmas drink.

Souse .... Dish made from pork, pig souse.

Sparrow .... Slinger Francisco, Calypso King.

Split de scene .... To leave, go away in a hurry.

Tassa .... East Indian drums.

Thru .... Through.

TELCO .... Telephone Company.

Ticker .... Thicker.
Tinkin' .... Thinking.
U.W.I. .... University of the West Indies.
WASA .... Water and Sewerage Authority.
Wassy .... Everything's fine, feeling good.
Who vex loss .... Couldn't care less, to not give a damn.
Woulda .... Would have.
Wuk .... Work.